Advance Praise

"*EPIC!* is an extraordinary book filled with the wisdom and practices to design your most exquisite life. I've had the great fortune of knowing Carolyn Buck Luce for many years, and she's a remarkable, engaging, and gifted leader. She's created one of the most powerful coaching tools that I've ever experienced—the Decade Game—to help women heal themselves, manifest their highest contributions, and change the world! Read this book and discover how."

—MARCI SHIMOFF, *New York Times* bestselling author of *Happy for No Reason*

"Carolyn is a powerful leader and brilliant teacher who ignites the best in others. Her book, *EPIC!*, is a must-read for women who are ready to step into their full power. Now is the time to bring Venus and Mars into full harmony."

—DR. JOHN GRAY, bestselling author of *Men Are from Mars, Women Are from Venus*

"What could be more important than designing your own life for what you truly want? What could be more engaging than turning it into a game? In this inspiring and deeply useful guide, Carolyn Buck Luce, a remarkably wise and compassionate leader with wide-ranging experience in the real world,

invites us on a life-changing journey to get to YES with ourselves. What a priceless gift!"
—WILLIAM URY, world-renowned negotiation expert and co-author of *Getting to Yes*

"Women's leadership is essential to address the moral and existential challenges of the future. *EPIC!* was written for such a time as this! Through her own experiences and mentoring thousands of women, Carolyn Buck Luce has honed the methodology and play-full practices to help women to discover their own purpose, power, and potential for good. This book is essential and guides each of us in our contribution that collectively can advance a world of justice and love."
—REV. DR. KATHARINE R. HENDERSON, President Emerita of Auburn Seminary

"The Decade Game described in *EPIC!* came at a pivotal time for me—ten years after launching my second career. The game is helping me get clarity on what would be truly authentic and energizing contributions to my clients and community and areas of personal growth for me to enable those contributions. I would highly recommend it."
—HENNA INAM, Executive Coach, Independent Board Director, author of *Wired for Disruption*

"The power plays of clarifying my Stand, destination, and pillars gave me not only valuable perspective for weighing and designing future options, but also confidence in observing

how past choices and outcomes implicitly connected to these guiding themes."
—LORI ROSENKOPF, Vice Dean of Entrepreneurship at the Wharton School

"The wisdom and power tools of the Decade Game helped me to understand and connect the most fundamental things about myself—in some ways, I feel like I clicked myself into place and am now feeling such a sense of 'Ahhhhh.'"
—TERRI POLLEY, former President and CEO of Financial Accounting Foundation

"I am so grateful that I dedicated the time and myself to this experience. It has created a sense of purpose, calm, and confidence that I have longed for. I can't wait to dominate my next decade."
—LAURIE KOWALEVSKY, CMO, Lilly Biomedicines at Eli Lilly

"The insights and power of *EPIC!* and the roadmap of the Decade Game have been absolutely transformational. They provided me with a relevant, thoughtful, and actionable framework for focusing on my purpose. They helped me think bigger and challenge myself to be my best self."
—LISA SHALETT, former Goldman Sachs partner; Board Director; Co-Founder, Extraordinary Women on Boards

"Whose game am I playing? The answer had rarely been clear and was too often 'not mine.' The power of *EPIC!* has focused my power, streamlined my thinking, and solidified my vision and intentions. I now know who I am, where I am going, and find the path unfurling before me in surprising ways that I am ready to fully engage with. It is hard work made fun, deep work made pleasurable, and transformation made sustainable. To bring your light, rock this world, and create a mind-blowing future—get in the game!"

—TIFFANY VARA, activist and philanthropist

"*EPIC!* is a must-read, and the Decade Game is a brilliant way to engage with creating an empowering and powerful future and vision for your life. With many approaches available for doing this, the created future can seem like a mere hoped-for but unlikely pipe dream. Not so here! The vision becomes palpable, alive, and breathing and begins to alter how you see and experience your everyday present. All of a sudden, you find yourself naturally making choices that lead toward the new future—engaging in new practices, having different conversations, putting unexpected and exciting things in your calendar, all of which are easy, effortless steps to fulfilling your vision."

—DEBBIE KING, Principal and Owner,
Transformational Leadership Partners

"*EPIC!* is a gift. The wisdom of the Decade Game offered me the opportunity to dive deep, dream big, assess wisely, and set clear intentions about the direction of my life. It's such a brilliant way to get really clear about what makes your soul sing! As a result, I'm better oriented toward my desires and am enjoying a clarity about the actions that are in alignment with those desires and which ones are not. *EPIC!* is where you go to stop playing games and start playing BIG."

—AKILAH RICHARDS, author, organizer, podcaster

"The Decade Game is life-altering in every way. It inspired me to take a whole new level of responsibility for my life. Standing in a decade from now getting 'here from there' rather than 'there from here' changed my whole framing, outlook, and perspective from a tenuous 'Can I..?' to a powerful 'I already have...' The process is spectacular, empowering, clarifying, and incredibly effective. I recommend it to anyone of any age or any stage of life. Go for it. It will not just change your life—it will empower you to create it!"

—LYNNE TWIST, author of *The Soul of Money*,
President, The Soul of Money Institute, Co-founder,
Pachamama Alliance

"*EPIC!* is truly for everyone. Entrepreneurs, young professionals, seasoned corporate managers, leaders, parents, and artists alike. The unique Decade Game is one of the most powerful tools you can implement in your work, your life, and your journey. If you are serious about living into your fullest potential, this is the next essential Step toward actualizing your purpose."

—TASHA MOFFITT, Executive Producer,
The Wahl Group Inc.

"Read this book and learn to play the Decade Game. It was a game-changer for me. Looking ten years into my future was exhilarating! The inspiring stories and power tools helped me get clear about what I was passionate about: health, healing, science, learning, and working with people who have a common purpose. I now have a vision of my future and a foundational game board which leaves space for magic to happen."

—CHERYL BUCK, Founder and Chief Vision Officer, CancerTalks

"*EPIC!* is a one-of-a-kind intellectual, emotional, spiritual deep dive that superpowers your innate gifts. With compassion and empathy, Carolyn deftly leads you on a soulful journey of self-inquiry that results in the creation of your own powerful, personal Decade Game®—where you design the future of your dreams, and then you make it happen. It is a game where everyone wins, and it is brilliant fun to play."

—KIM MORTON, artist and activist

"As a high-performing woman of color, I never quite realized how much my 'inherited' limiting beliefs were getting in the way of my dreams. Carolyn's Decade Game® has a magical way of getting straight to the Truth of our soul's desire. Playing the Decade Game® has helped me confront the internal roadblocks and resistance to creating the big life that I am meant to live. It has also showed me that it can be deliciously fun to design our own unique and powerful imprint on the World."

—VANESSA BRADLEY, investor and philanthropist

"Ten years from now, what life or world-changing transformations could you catalyze with your superpowers if you were not afraid? Throughout *EPIC!* Carolyn Buck Luce applies her evolving shamanic wisdom to help us declare what we stand for and to design a dynamic roadmap to make it happen. This work has and continues to profoundly alter my own professional and personal destination."

—TERI RIDDLE, CEO, The Crossland Group

"The Decade Game is a transformative experience, regardless of where your starting line is or what path you're currently on. Whether you're looking to drive forward into discovering and realizing goals that you've been holding back, or you need to give yourself the permission to walk away from all the 'shoulds' that have crept into your world, you'll have the time, structure, and support from an amazing group of humans who are all invested in helping you visualize and create your best, most purposeful life."

—VAL MORINI, Director, Wells Fargo

"*EPIC!* is a treasure chest of practical wisdom. The meta 'play' in this essential book is the Decade Game, which allowed me to let go of the past and fully face and imagine an exciting future that is bigger and brighter than I could have imagined before. This is one of the greatest gifts you can give yourself or any accomplished female leader you admire."

—MICHELLE BOTTOMLEY, Fortune 50 Executive
and Independent Board Member

EPIC!

EPIC!

THE WOMEN'S
Power
Play Book

CAROLYN BUCK LUCE

LIONCREST
PUBLISHING

Hardcover ISBN: 978-1-5445-3049-9
Paperback ISBN: 978-1-5445-3050-5
Ebook ISBN: 978-1-5445-3051-2

For the women who long to discover their destiny.

For the sisters who have inspired my EPIC journey.

And to my husband Rob,
who walks with me every step of the way.

Contents

Foreword

By Lynne Twist

The book you hold in your hands will empower you to be the woman you've always dreamed of being in every aspect of your life. The work that Carolyn has done to create this book began when she was eight years old and decided to take her future self into her own hands guided by her own sense of purpose and an innovative process she invented, now known as the Decade Game. Throughout her remarkable life, she has continued to discover a deeper and more powerful version of herself, becoming more and more true to her life's purpose.

Having worked closely with Carolyn over the past decade, I have found her to be one of the most self-assured, gifted, and high-achieving women I've ever known. She is a brilliant strategist and leader who has spent her career building highly effective cultures, businesses, and teams. Diplomat, Wall Street banker, management consultant, healthcare futurist, talent innovator, professor, author, philanthropist, executive coach, inventor of the Decade Game, Carolyn's journey has provided her with a unique perspective on thriving in a man's world.

What I love most about Carolyn is her deep spiritual life and devotion, as wife, mother, and grandmother, to her family, in addition to empowering and mentoring women. For the past five years, she has joined me in co-leading the Remarkable Women's Journey offered by The Soul of Money Institute, a six-month transformational program for women who are up to big things in the world. And that's what this book addresses: how women can step into their power and rightful role as leaders at this epic time in history.

I call this time the Sophia Century, the era when women will join in co-equal partnership with men and the world will come into balance. When women have a voice, when women are in the board room and at the peace table, and when women can bring heart, compassion, patience, and resilience into critical conversations and relationships, breakdowns can become breakthroughs. Today we face crises that no generation has seen before and possibilities that are almost unimaginable through yesterday's lens. We need to lead epic lives to meet them.

There is a beautiful teaching that comes from the Baha'i faith called "the bird of humanity." The bird has two great wings, one male and one female. The male wing has been fully outstretched for centuries, while the female wing has been folded in. The bird's male wing has become overdeveloped to keep itself afloat: its muscles strained, its movements violent. Without its balancing counterpart, the bird of humanity has been flying in circles, unable to reach the heights of real attainment.

The prophecy continues that the time must come for the female wing of the bird of humanity to fully extend itself and be expressed in all of us. Then the male wing can relax, find its healthy form, and, with two wings fully outstretched and of equivalent strength, the bird of humanity will soar to new heights.

This book is a contribution to that transformation. Carolyn's wisdom on living an EPIC! life is applicable for all people, but she has focused her attention primarily on women leaders. I am a witness to her teachings transforming the lives of countless women of all ages and stages. I have had extraordinary breakthroughs in my own leadership through the brilliance of her Decade Game process. When I turned seventy—a time when many people feel their life is declining—I, instead, was able to see the next ten years as the most powerful, productive, energetic, and healthy decade of my life.

I commend you for taking up this book and for your commitment to step into your power and purpose. It is the twenty-first-century power play book for women. Carolyn expresses her process as a game, which keeps it lighthearted, but it will have a profound transformational impact on your life. You will be encouraged to think and feel big and bold, in fact, EPIC! You will discover the tools to design a new game board that will guide you to live the best decade of your life so far. This book will not only be life-changing, it will also give you vitality, energy, and power that you may not have known before. As Carolyn says, "If you are not having fun, you are playing someone else's game."

You are in the capable hands of a woman who has lived and is living an epic life—the perfect guide to the next decade of your own epic life. Let the game begin!

Introduction

Living an epic life is a choice. Seriously. It's a choice you
can make today, regardless of your circumstances. Let's
pause on this word, "epic." When I first mention this scary
four-letter word to women, I feel their insides clutching up.
Let me be clear. I am not talking about our current culture of
"more is better" and the insatiable desire to be richer, more
successful, thinner, more famous, more everything in a race to
be King of the Hill. I am in search of a more feminine, wholis-
tic, spiritual construct that guides us toward a commitment
and clarity to get to the center of our most authentic self, in
deep communion with others and the natural world. I am on
the hunt for the human being, not the human doing. In this
context, epic-ness is available to you—regardless of your age,
your level of wealth, your race, or your family conditions.

We each know who we really are when we are our best
self and not afraid—loving, hopeful, creative, compassionate, faithful, nonjudgmental, longing for possibilities. At
our essence, we each have the assets and attributes we need
to design a life of meaning and purpose. We can choose to

discover meaning for ourselves in whatever life throws at us and, at the same time, create meaning for others. We can own that life is happening "for us," not "to us."

I know you know this. Do you remember playing "make-believe" as a child? I do. My mother's wedding dress had a name—"sea foam over dawn"—a profusion of swishy sea green chiffon over a blush dawn silk sheath. When I put that dress on, I was transformed. The make-believe game was magical as long as the dress was on.

Here is the secret to an epic life. Turn the rest of your life into a make-believe game. Get equipped with the tools of a great game developer to play a game of your own design. One that is worth spending your entire life playing. Creating an epic life is a multifaceted challenge, but like all games worth playing—the harder the challenge, the more fun we need to have to play our heart out.

Games are designed to be epic. You purchase a game for its longed-for objective—fame, fortune, love, peace, adventure, discovery. The more marvelous the objective, the more fun to play. Win or lose. Paradoxically, in the games we love to play again and again, there is no such thing as losing or a "last chance." If a move doesn't work out well, you jump in to play again—a little wiser. There is also no such thing as "a wrong move." There is only the next best move. Why shouldn't life be like that? Why not live a life of curiosity and adventure, redesigning the rules to fit your unique circumstances?

I moved on from the make-believe games of early childhood when I was eight and experienced my first live superhero. This discovery launched me from a self-absorbed child into a baby citizen with a wider worldview. It was the fall of 1960, and John F. Kennedy was running for president against Richard Nixon. I was mesmerized by JFK, who seemed like a shining knight to me. He was very clear about what he expected of all citizens: "Ask not what your country can do for you; ask what you can do for your country." A moon shot. A Peace Corp. Wow. I wanted to be just like him—a world leader committed to making the world better. At that age, well-versed in fairy tales, magical legends, and mythic stories of gods and goddesses, I felt touched by destiny and began to imagine how an epic life would unfold, with me as the heroine of my own story. That episode birthed the first version of my Decade Game, which I have been designing and playing ever since.

In this power play book, I will introduce you to the Decade Game framework, share the stories and secrets of women who are playing for the epic win of meaning and purpose, and guide you to design your own game with your own rules. The Decade Game is a continual practice of make-believe. You are both the designer and the player of a game with an epic quest. The magic of your design is that it continues to evolve as life unfolds, integrating all parts of your life. You will learn to build the scaffolding that supports your commitment to mastery and brilliance in your personal, professional, and philanthropic life. You will discover what is longing to happen for you at each stage of your life's journey. You will be able to finally answer these questions:

- How do I recover my most unique, authentic self—and be true to her?
- How do I let go of the beliefs that no longer serve me?
- How do I find the clarity for what *really* is my spiritual and material work in this world?
- How can I be confident that the next decade can be the best decade of my life so far?
- How do I recover when an unexpected trap door opens, and I fall through?

These vital questions require a customized answer. This is no off-the-shelf fix, "Follow this ten-step journey to fulfillment." The Decade Game honors the labyrinthine path of our lives and guides us to the heart of the matter. If there's a rung on the "career" ladder worth climbing, we'll learn to recognize it, and of course—we'll climb. But the Decade Game is designed for your mind, body, heart, and soul transformation—to get to the center, not the top. And that journey is truly epic. A game worth playing for dear life.

My own epic journey has taken me into the halls of power in the masculine world of diplomacy, international banking, Wall Street deal-making, and management consulting. In these rooms, I learned the art of strategy, negotiation, persuasion, presence, and performance. It has also invited me at the same time into the heart of womanhood as a wife, mother, and grandmother. In this place, I have experienced the awesome majesty of being the birther, the nurturer, and the mourner. And I am quite sure about this. Women are born to be leaders at home and in society, regardless of whether they are getting a paycheck for their efforts.

Throughout most of this journey, I felt I was on my own, feeling my way. The literature and advice seemed 100 percent half right. How to do it all. How to have it all. Lean in. Work/Life balance. Toot your horn. Get the corner office. The essence of the teaching was how to compete head-to-head in a man's world and win. However, what I was observing, for myself and for the women I worked with, was that women's true gifts were vastly undervalued, and our aspirations were deeply diminished, to the detriment of all. Although I could win with the best of them at work, I believed my "real" job was operating as an "agent provocateur" behind enemy lines. As a mentor and sponsor of other women, I was working heart-to-heart, leading the charge for women's ability to navigate the black box of power and ambition—without losing themselves. All this, while traversing the joys and tragedies of a woman's life, blending three families with six children through three marriages, one ending with divorce and another ending with the death of my second husband.

I have taken this real job to heart. It started with mentoring many women I worked with about how I played the game my way, sharing my Decade Game framework. This led me to create a course—The Practicum on Women and Power, which I taught for a decade at Columbia University's Graduate School of International Affairs and Public Policy—for full-time graduate students committed to changing the world. Since matriculating (i.e., mandatory retirement!) at sixty from my partnership at Ernst & Young LLP, a global professional services firm, I have continued to "stir the pot" to help women acknowledge, embrace, and activate their epic-ness in all areas of their lives. These days I have been blessed to work with a few of my favorite epic women in co-designing and co-leading The Decade Game Master Class and incorporating the game into the intensive six-month Remarkable Women's Journey.

Come on this journey with me to recover your EPIC! self and discover your destiny.

Section I

Life by Design

"This is a very interesting time: there are no models for anything that is going on. Everything is changing, even the law of the masculine jungle. It is a period of free fall into the future, and each has to make his or her own way. The old models are not working; the new have not yet appeared. In fact, it is we who are even now shaping the new in the shaping of our interesting lives. And that is the whole sense (in mythological terms) of the present challenge: **we are the 'ancestors' of an age to come**, the unwitting generators of its supporting myths, the mythic models that will inspire its lives."

—JOSEPH CAMPBELL,
from *Goddesses: Mysteries of the Feminine Divine*

Chapter 1

Let the
Game Begin

Once upon a time...

When I was forty-nine, I was on the cusp of being promoted to vice chairman at my company, Ernst & Young LLP ("EY"), or so I thought. Already a partner for over a decade, I'd had an amazing run at the company—mostly in positions entirely of my own design as I was originally hired to help launch new businesses. As a woman in corporate America since the late seventies, I had learned the hard way that I would be passed over for competitive, sought-after promotions. The fastest way to the top was to put your hand up for the difficult or not-yet existent businesses. For the past decade, I had done just that, building new product revenue streams and innovative businesses that pushed us outside of our traditional swim lanes. One of my favorite "game moves" was volunteering to lead our e-commerce strategy in the early days of the internet when Amazon was a startup bookseller and before we had heard of Google and Facebook. (Remember Netscape?) You get the idea.

My professional reviews were glowing, and my direct reporting relationship with the company president was solid. I thought the next step was clear—company vice chairman, just like the title of the other three direct reports to the president. I had already bought some vice chairman–inspired outfits. I was ready. Then, the hidden trap door opened, and I fell through. Not all the innovative ideas they asked me to pursue were working out as hoped. Some top leaders didn't have a long history with me and didn't really "get" me. It turns out support for me was icy thin.

Glass ceilings are tricky. The cliché holds true-to-form because, like glass, You. Can. Never. See. It—until it smacks you hard in the head. To add insult to injury, you can see the faces looking through the glass observing your slip-up, but no hands are reaching through from the top to offer you a lifeline!

Of course, this doesn't happen only in business. Sometimes you look up at your perfect life with your husband, Labrador, and two-and-a-half kids and find yourself stuck in a glass cage of your own making. All the wine and wishful thinking in the world won't change the claustrophobic parameters of that crystalline jewelry box. We can't predict what will happen—and even the most epic decade of your life won't be without its curves and detours—even its tragedies, illnesses, and loss, all of which I have experienced.

Back to the backstory. There I was, at forty-nine years old, nursing a new and completely unexpected head wound. How had I missed it? I'm a strategist and consider myself an expert in women's leadership. I was even one of the founding members of our chairman's pioneering gender equity task force set up in the early 1990s. Having been shocked at my glass ceiling, I needed to find out why I hadn't seen it coming. I investigated. I requested meetings with all the senior members (mostly men) of the management committee. I asked them for genuine feedback. As I made the rounds, it was like the Goldilocks fairy tale repeated over and over. "You're too this, Carolyn. You're too that. Not quite right. Too independent, too competitive, too assertive, too articulate, too educated. You're not vulnerable enough. Not sure you are a team player." My favorite feedback was from another vice chairman who said, "You are like the seven-foot basketball player—you were the first draft pick, and then we kept you on the bench because we didn't like the way you shot the ball." The very attributes I had flexed to be the innovator and builder of new businesses in a traditional culture were now being held against me. A woman acting too much like a man goes against the expected archetype and is at best not trusted and at worst...

When I went home at the end of that week, I couldn't pretend I didn't feel hurt, angry, upset, underappreciated, undervalued, underestimated, and shoved out. It would have been easy to take it personally and answer one of the calls I frequently received from executive search firms. But I had learned over the years that my ambition and success were my responsibility, my game. As someone who started her career as a diplomat in the Soviet Union in the mid-seventies, I knew to approach work as a cultural anthropologist, studying how each organization's culture informed who the "in-laws and the outlaws" were. In male-dominated professions like diplomacy, investment banking, and management consulting, I was always the outlaw. I often experienced exclusion in my forty-plus-year career, starting when I was rejected from every college on the first try (having spent more time on revolution and rock and roll than apparently was useful). I had learned to anticipate what I call the "ABCs" of my life—Anyone But Carolyn.

A good rule-of-thumb that I have used to navigate the ABCs (both personally and professionally) is: when it comes to culture, everybody is guilty, but no one's to blame. It's too easy and lazy to blame others for not understanding you and your worth. There is always an important truth buried in feedback. The management committee of my firm had an experience of me that was true for them. My most important takeaway was that my colleagues didn't truly know who I was, what I did, or why I did it. They didn't appreciate that for women to be successful in the last half of the twentieth century, they had to be "know-it-alls." Never asking for help. Showing they could do it against all odds. I had assumed that my excellent performance and willingness to tackle even the toughest problems would speak for itself. I had bet on meritocracy. Seen through the lens of culture, I saw that this disconnect was my misstep to fix. The reality is that those in the minority always shoulder the burden of making the majority comfortable. It was time to lay out the game board for my next decade and figure out my next best move.

That Sunday after church, I waited until my kids were doing homework and, after having preached a great sermon, my husband was in the living room, entertained by a football game. I poured myself a fragrant mug of my favorite hazelnut coffee, sat down at my romantic kitchen nook in my New York City apartment, and took a few big sips. I had remodeled the open space living room and kitchen to look like an outdoor café and piazza in Florence so that every time I sat there, I could imagine myself in Renaissance Italy. I had even brought in a set designer to make twelve-foot-high faux marble pillars that accentuated the floor-to-ceiling windows with a killer view. Every time I nestled into this nook and looked out at the manifestation of my imagination, I was transported to another time and space that jump-started my future dreaming.

I took a deep breath. I had been complacent, lured by the promise of a promotion that would shout, "She has arrived!" I had defaulted into playing someone else's game—a masculine, corporate game at which I was extremely adept but could never, ever win. You can lean in all the way as a woman or outsider and still lose. Living an EPIC! life is about liberation. Free of the box. Free of the ceiling. Free of all the elements, glass and otherwise, that diminish our ability as women to be the leaders we know we can be—at home, at work, and in our communities. It is important to understand that there is no loser in this game. As the designer, you have the power to construct a game where everyone wins—you, your loved ones, your organization, your community, and the future.

I took out my paper and a pen and began to play a game I had played before—the Decade Game. I sketched out the game board that would take me from fifty to sixty (the company's mandatory retirement age). That initial sketch became my lifeline for a great, tumultuous, surprising, taxing, heart-breaking, rewarding, and utterly memorable decade. Although, at the time, I had no idea of the multitude of permutations and surprises that would emerge over the decade, the aspirational outlines of this dream board did not change.

Here is that game board. Don't worry right now about the details and rules of how to play the game. By the end of this book, I will equip you with the insights and "how-tos" needed to design your own initial game board and playbook for the most epic decade of your life. For now, just feel the longing for spiritual, relational, professional, and philanthropic growth that is being expressed and the dynamic transformational trajectory from year one to year ten.

Let me emphasize that the goal of the Decade Game is not to realize your exact epic dreams but, rather, to be willing to have them. By owning your power and promise, you are better guided and equipped to reach for the experiences, knowledge, skills, and relationships that would make you capable of EPIC! outcomes. It is in the presence of these dreams that you will find purpose. And magic can happen. In fact, in 2012, the last year of that Decade Game, I was able to look back in amazement at what had happened:

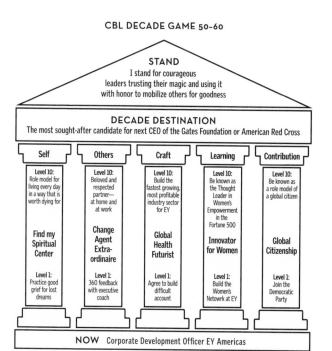

CBL DECADE GAME 50-60

STAND
I stand for courageous
leaders trusting their magic and using it
with honor to mobilize others for goodness

DECADE DESTINATION
The most sought-after candidate for next CEO of the Gates Foundation or American Red Cross

Self	Others	Craft	Learning	Contribution
Level 10: Role model for living every day in a way that is worth dying for	Level 10: Beloved and respected partner— at home and at work	Level 10: Build the fastest growing, most profitable industry sector for EY	Level 10: Be known as the Thought Leader in Women's Empowerment in the Fortune 500	Level 10: Be known as a role model of a global citizen
Find my Spiritual Center	**Change Agent Extraordinaire**	**Global Health Futurist**	**Innovator for Women**	**Global Citizenship**
Level 1: Practice good grief for lost dreams	Level 1: 360 feedback with executive coach	Level 1: Agree to build difficult account	Level 1: Build the Women's Netowrk at EY	Level 1: Join the Democratic Party

NOW   Corporate Development Officer EY Americas

- Built a successful $1 billion Global Life Sciences business at EY.
- Named Woman of the Year by the Healthcare Businesswomen's Association.
- Elected Chairwoman of the NY Women's Foundation.
- Appointed by Mayor Bloomberg to his NYC Commission on Women's Issues.
- Co-founded the nonprofit think tank, The Center for Talent Innovation (now Coqual).
- Published several articles in the Harvard Business Review on gender equity and inclusion.
- Served as an adjunct professor at Columbia, teaching my Practicum on Women and Power.

It turns out that people dramatically overestimate what they can get done in a year and exponentially underestimate what they can accomplish in a decade.

An epic life is not just about a career. Nor does it only come with victories. It is about living intensely, being in the moment, taking nothing for granted, striving to be your best self. It turns out the most significant event came four years into my game, at age fifty-four. A surprise trap door flew open with a terminal cancer diagnosis for my husband when he was fifty-seven. My major focus shifted for the next three years as I shepherded Forrest to a good death and supported his and my children through that journey. I couldn't have predicted that after experiencing a broken heart, at the end of that Decade Game, the week after I retired from EY, I was able to give my heart away again and marry Rob Evans.

At fifty, sitting in my Florence-inspired kitchen, sipping my coffee, and sketching my game board, I had sparked an imaginal process that would transform the next ten years of my life. Metamorphosis. We all grew up knowing a bit about the metamorphosis of a caterpillar into a butterfly. The mind-boggling part of this process is the biologic detail of how it happens. After a period of ravenous consumption, a caterpillar finds an appropriate perch and forms a chrysalis— so far, so good. The result is a butterfly. The astonishing truth is that there is no cellular similarity at all between a caterpillar and a butterfly. Inside the chrysalis, the caterpillar—unable to move—secretes digestive enzymes that begin to dissolve itself into an organic "goop" to feed what is about to become. There is a knowing that is about to awaken, which has lain dormant in the caterpillar since its beginning pupal stage—biologists call this knowing "imaginal cells."

In biology, "imago" is the adult form an insect takes in the last stage of metamorphosis. This mature stage is called the imaginal stage. At first, these imaginal cells, like stem cells, have their own unique identity and operate independently as single-cell organisms. Structurally, they resemble neither caterpillar nor butterfly cells, yet they hold the seeds of future potential. They have the knowing, which contains the blueprint of a flying creature. The imaginal cells are regarded as threats and are attacked by the caterpillar's immune system. But they persist, multiply, and connect with each other. The cells cluster into clumps and begin resonating at the same frequency. Information is passed back and forth until the clumps reach an integrative tipping point—and a butterfly is born.

We humans also have a deep knowing about what is longing to happen. We were conceived with it—an imaginal knowing of what is possible when we are connected to our power and aligned with a life-long purpose. We know it intuitively as children, filled with possibilities in a world of make-believe. Just believing is enough to make it real—emotionally, somatically, and spiritually. Then we forget—filling ourselves with imaginary stories of who we need to be to belong, to be loved, and to be safe. The reality is we don't live in our lives. We live in the stories we tell and believe about ourselves and others.

Here is a truer, generative, awe-inspiring story. We, as imaginal human cells, have in our nature the ability to dream, sense, envision, intuit, and almost taste the unprecedented possibilities that might be emerging in the near or distant future, and these intuitions can be lived into now. We, who create life for others, have the imaginal knowing of how to create a magnificent life for ourselves, based on an individual and unique design, guided by that which is greater than all yet present in each.

Contemplate this—no person in history has ever had the same fingerprint that you do. Given technological advancements, we now know that no one who has ever lived has the same eye pigmentation as you. No one who has ever walked on this planet has the identical vocal timbre as you. This means that your way of doing, your perspective in how you see the world, and the truth you can voice are unique to you. You have all the powers of the universe to create a life by design, not default.

Unlike the imago, the adult insect, our species is "*Homo sapiens*," which means "the wise one." We are born with the deep knowing of the metamorphosis that is awaiting each of us. We have imaginal agency that allows us to choose and strive to manifest our most authentic, unique form. We can lean into what is longing to happen, to say "yes" to our becoming, fueled by the feminine knowledge of creation that has been passed down to us and through us over the millennia.

There is a voice of longing, an imaginal knowing, inside each woman. We strive so mightily to be good: good partners, daughters, mothers, employees, and friends. As accomplished and loving women, we have filled our life with plans and projects. We hope all this striving will make us feel that we have done great work. Goals, lists, to-dos, deadlines. It's hard work to manage all the commitments that we have made to so many. It's even harder to imagine what is possible in ten years when we can't think past what needs to be done in the next ten minutes. Instead of excitement over the endless possibilities that the future holds, our promises leave us feeling weary, stuck, overwhelmed with the tasks, and at the same time underwhelmed in our souls. We are haunted by questions like, "Is there more?" Women of all ages and at all stages want more, and YET we think we can get more only by giving more and giving up more. How ironic that in using our instinct for nurturing others, we misuse our commitment to our own becoming.

This deep inquiry happened so many times in the two decades I was a partner at EY. I still have the meetings in my dreams. Like clockwork, a brilliant young woman—a global consultant or financial analyst—would send me an email requesting a private meeting. A quick review of her profile would show her as a rising star, an incredible asset to the company, a fierce talent with glowing reviews. Usually, she'd be a self-starter, her ambition and ability clear from her top performance in everything she touched. EY was meticulous in spotting and recruiting the best talent and bringing them into our fold. The young corporate women knocking on my office door were the best of the best. Nonetheless, I knew to have the tissue box close at hand.

It takes guts to request an audience with a partner, particularly for women who try to show they can do it all on their own. EY worked hard to be a cordial, encouraging place to work. Yet, it was still a part of the elite professional partnership world. Hyper-masculine energy prevailed, with relentless, comparative competition and a lot of swagger. Partnership structures, like corporate hierarchies, are based on most people not making partner or being promoted to the executive ranks. Rocking the boat and admitting any weakness by requesting an audience to expose vulnerability and doubt with a partner is a high-risk/low return strategy.

I always welcomed the women with a smile, watched them take in and adjust to the vibrant colors and bold artwork of my office. I had a reputation for handling the "master of the universe" world of corporate power like a champ, but my office was a distinctly feminine space—indicative of my comfort level with my own power. Festooned with pictures of my kids, adventure photos with my husband, large plants, and a bold, wall-sized painting created for me by my sister-in-law entitled "Possibilities II," my office was a statement to my commitment to be a leader at home, at work, and in the world. Here is the scene:

Nervously, the young woman would take her seat across from me. I'd ask her a few questions about her latest deal or project, some small talk to make her comfortable.

"What can I do for you?" I'd finally ask.

"I just…I love my job. I'm good at it. But I'm having some doubts." By this time, tears would be imminent, and I would slide the Kleenex box across the desk.

"Doubts about what?" I'd ask—though I knew.

"Doubts about my future. About the partner track. I worked for this my entire life. I'm driven. I'm focused. I'm excellent at what I do. But I'm just not sure…I'm not sure I want to be a partner."

My response was always the same.

"Why don't you tell me about the partner you don't want to be? Because I bet I wouldn't want to be that partner either."

Here is the dilemma. It didn't matter how successful and brilliant the young analyst on the opposite side of my desk was. Like many women and historically underrepresented talent in corporate America, she was playing a game that rewarded the dominant white masculine archetype of what a leader should look like, act like, and care about. Success in this environment requires molding oneself into the accepted and expected pattern—an impossible task for anyone who doesn't fit the traditional mold. The effort to bridge this gap can be exhausting and soul-crushing—and leave even the most talented, ambitious people ambivalent about their futures. Success feels like the burden that will keep on growing, and a career that started with a commitment to thrive becomes merely a test to survive.

But what if there was a different view of what leadership looks and feels like? Consistently at my Women and Power Practicum at Columbia, my time at EY, my current work with Berkeley's Hass Business School's Women's Executive Leadership Program, and in my group coaching work with women, I witness the miracle of metamorphosis when women can write the real story of their dreams, power, and purpose. By imagining the powerhouse they long to be, their "If Only" story shifts to the epic saga of "Imagine If." The butterfly is liberated. The imaginal cells in us awaken, cluster, and find each other.

We women are being called to put aside the self-limiting fears of letting people down, of not being loved, of not being perfect, of not being enough. Metamorphosis is hard work, particularly when the patriarchal, privileged culture we exist in is unamicable and, oftentimes, hostile to women's power and ambition. We are still playing "not to lose" as opposed to playing to win. We are bit players in a game designed to have us stay within the lines of the approved script. It is time to break free from the cocoon.

Transformation can take years—and sometimes, when you are ready, it can happen in a minute. ***The real power of the Decade Game is that it doesn't take ten years to feel its EPIC! impact. It can happen in an afternoon. And it can start right now.*** You don't have to wait for your "chronological" decade. Nothing new must be learned, no experiences must be acquired, no new resources are needed, no money need be exchanged, no new adventures are necessary. All you need to do is say "yes" to what you are longing for. Feel fully empowered to be all that you can be. Say "yes" to your body. Play full out in meaningful ways that can make a difference, no matter how small. Stop playing tiny and speaking softly. No longer downsize your truth or dim the light of your talent. Name what you wish for that you are willing to work for. Say what, deep down, you know to be true. "I am a gift! It's time to open the present."

In her magnificent foreword, Lynne Twist welcomed us into the Sophia Century. This is the century and the decade that is calling on all women to step up and take their rightful place with men to bring forth an environmentally sustainable, socially just, spiritually fulfilling human presence on this planet. We are being summoned to be powerful on purpose.

We are being encouraged to rewrite the fairy tales that limited our characters' plots and adventures. When we do this, we have the recipe for an EPIC! life—one that is worth dying for.

My greatest desire for this book is to gift you the inspiration, insights, clarity, confidence, tools, and support to design an original playbook that will guide you in uncovering your purpose, recovering your power, and discovering your destiny. This is the game you've been waiting to play all your life. I'm so thrilled to play with you.

Game ON!

Rules of the Game:
Create a life by design, not default.

Chapter 2

The Stories We're Told

One afternoon, my son Jake, then seven, came into my study to speak with me, insisting that I drop everything and get him the class list from school with everyone's phone numbers. When asked what he wanted it for, it turned out that everyone at school, he said, was talking about Danny's birthday party. EVERYONE. And he hadn't been invited.

He wasn't so much upset as bewildered. "Mom, why wasn't I invited? Do you think his mom forgot? Maybe they don't have our number or lost the class list? Or maybe he thought I didn't want to come. I need to call him and let him know I would like to be invited!" He was already heading to the phone.

The audacity of little boys! His response—logical though it was—made me deeply uncomfortable. It went against all my acculturated conditioning. I had to stop myself from calling him back into the study to explain that it wasn't polite to call about a party you weren't invited to. I remember my mother soothing me as I cried my eyes out in elementary school when I was left out of the fun. Bereft at the time, I was sure I would never have another friend. My son's reaction made perfect logical sense. He had no self-doubt about the appropriate course of action to remedy the problem. He had every confidence in his own value—and every confidence that others would be able to see it.

And he was right. Twenty minutes later, Jake had his invitation.

Like so many women, I was raised to be a "Good Girl," to shrink myself to fit society's expectations. To not be too loud, too assertive, too bold, too noticeable, too MUCH. I have found that this is a universal phenomenon. No matter where I have traveled in the world, I ask women the same question. "Who was raised to be a Good Girl?" Whether I am in Minneapolis, Mumbai, Mexico City, or Moscow—almost everyone's hand shoots up with no hesitation. Although the story differs from place to place, every woman on the planet knows what that means.

It goes something like this:

- Good Girls shouldn't be too ambitious.
- Good Girls watch what they eat.
- Good Girls shouldn't speak up.
- Good Girls don't invite themselves to the party.
- Good Girls can dream big as long as they play small.

Why? So that we would be liked, loved, approved of...
and safe.

It never crossed my son's mind that if he wanted something, he shouldn't just ask. Nor did it occur to him that he would be unloved if he did ask. Unlike a "Good Girl," if he was refused, it wasn't personal. My son doesn't have the running narrative in his head that almost every woman from every culture I have ever met has—it is the Good Girl story.

This Good Girl narrative is the embodiment of the thousands of little stories that we were told and then learned to tell ourselves about how girls should think, behave, look, and speak. Our observations and our direct experience of the consequences for women and girls who color outside the lines have constantly reinforced this narrative. Research shows that girls begin to adapt their behavior and responses to please others by age eight or nine. They are already aware, even if unconsciously, of the various incentives for being a Good Girl—and of the consequences of stepping outside that tiny box. The dread of these consequences runs deep.

Even though I know this, it always breaks my heart when I hear how embodied the vein of fear and trauma is in women who have a story in their bones about not being "good enough." Here are some "I am not a good enough" stories from women that strangle EPIC! These women are leaders in business, philanthropy, and the arts, all of whom are accomplished, remarkable, powerful, committed, determined women—and yet even they believe the following:

- I am unlovable and/or unlovely.
- Others are more important than me.
- No matter how hard I try, it's never enough.
- It is not safe to speak my truth.
- I am not brave.
- I am not warm enough, too intimidating.
- I am selfish to want more.

There are many things that Good Girls can't be. I believe at the top of the "no-no' list for women is to be "too ambitious." Why is ambition such a dirty word? Ambition is just another word for one's desire to accomplish. This desire is one of the distinct characteristics that differentiates us from other sentient beings. The longing to accomplish is the natural fuel to learn and grow.

Here's the problem. Good Girls have been venturing out into the world in droves for the last half century, manifesting their desire to be the leaders they long to be. The very qualities required for success in the "outside" world—desire, drive, and stepping into one's power to achieve your purpose—require them to "be bad" and act outside the norm expected of them. This creates a vicious cycle where women must push themselves beyond their Good Girl stories—and the more they do, the more pushback they get from a world that is ambivalent about women exercising power and claiming ambition.

Unfortunately, the patriarchal norms that we navigate have been around for 5,000 years and aren't going away soon. I'm forever haunted by that Newsweek cover during Hilary Clinton's presidential run. Politics aside, it was a horrific caricature where the artist had transformed this brilliant, bold, and yes, ambitious politician into a hairy, muscled, male athlete—replete with a bulging jock strap. The message was clear: assert your power as an ambitious woman, and be ridiculed, despised—and worse, in danger. In 2021, we elected the first woman vice president who had to fight through the smears of being "too ambitious." This narrative contributed to tanking her own presidential run.

This vicious cycle comes in the form of another archetypal story, which I mentioned in Chapter 1. Do you remember the fairy tale of Goldilocks? She is the adventurous little girl who goes into the woods to explore—where girls were not supposed to enter alone. Uninvited, she enters the hut of the Three Bears and messes with their stuff, trying to make herself at home. Everything she touches that belongs to the Mama and Papa bears—the beds, the chairs, the bowls of porridge—are "too this" or "too that," but never "just right." Only the baby bear's things are just right. But Goldilocks ruins them.

As our Good Girl ventures out into a man's world and experiments with ambition and power, she runs into the Goldilocks challenge, being deemed either "not enough" or "too much." (I am in the too much category.) But never "just right." For women pursuing an EPIC! life of power and purpose, it takes an incredible amount of strategy, energy, and grit to keep showing up when our Good Girl runs into Goldilocks. We are told to "lean in," yet the more we do, the trickier it gets. We need the skill of a runway model who can balance on a tightrope, twirling her parasol and ducking simultaneously from the constant curve balls being thrown her way.

I have had my own favorite Goldilocks feedback through-out my career—"too focused on my agenda," "too ambitious," "too strategic," "too 'smarty pants,'" "not vulnerable enough"— the list goes on. Because of how entrenched the Good Girl/ Goldilocks syndrome is in our culture, even the most accom-plished women fight self-doubts as to their own sufficiency. And it is a lifelong struggle. In the five years of trying to write what would be considered a "publishable" book (according to traditional publishers), it was hard not to lose heart. By potential agents and publishers alike, I was told to "dummy it down," "narrow my focus," "write at an eighth-grade level." In the end, I decided that this advice was antithetical to the core message of EPIC! and, instead, I accessed a less tradi-tional, hybrid route to market where I could say what was on my mind and heart. My way, my game.

It's important to know that "too little" or "too much" are two sides of the same coin. Either way, it always leads to giving away some of our power to make other people more comfortable. Think about it. Women have been trying to find their center whilst navigating this viscous cycle since child-hood. The cumulative impact creates a distorted relationship with power and ambition—we become power leakers in a way that drains our unique authenticity. Our attempts to manage this syndrome has our Good Girl persona settling for being good enough in our journey. Good enough is good but not sufficient. It is the antithesis to epic.

I have listened to hundreds of women committed to lead *epic lives* who have described how the Good Girl meets Goldilocks syndrome has solidified a "persona" that shapes and contains the way they show up in the world, to the det‑ riment of their aspirations and potential. They default to playing "not to lose." EPIC! requires playing for the multiple win—in all areas of your life.

Even though we women come in all shapes and sizes, all ages and stages, I have found that these personae fall into six major categories on the Goldilocks syndrome spectrum. When any of these personae hog the field of play, women are pushed out of playing their games and put into positions where they don't show up as their best, most powerful, and authentic self. Each persona gives up a lot. As you read through them, know that they are situational. You might find each resonates with you depending on the circumstance.

Starting with "I am too much" and moving down the spectrum:

Get the "A": A story of performance *at all costs*, knowing that you can climb any mountain and accomplish any challenge put in front of you. You are Ms. Responsibility, able to keep mul‑ tiple balls in the air *as long as you never*

stop juggling. You are struggling with how to be sure to make the right choices going forward. You wear your accomplishments like a medal of honor and are frustrated that meritocracy is not the abiding rule of the game. Your personal and spiritual lives suffer. And you are exhausted.

 **Dim My Light:** You know how talented you are, yet when you really shine, you are concerned that you will make others feel "less than." You are afraid that when you win, others lose. When you are enjoying your brightness, as you should, you are told you are "too much, too proud, too loud, too self-centered, too bossy." You feel misunderstood as to your intentions and underappreciated for your gifts. You are taught to be ashamed when you "hog the light." You can't share the joy of your victories. You do not feel fully seen or celebrated.

Imposter Syndrome: You can step up and show up to do the work in a man's world and prove your competency over and over. Yet you feel that you must be perfect to mask your doubts of not having the  right "stuff" and qualifications. You find it safer to be the #2 than push to be the #1 "Game Changer in Charge." You believe that your work, your voice, and your truth are not as important as your colleagues. You begin to doubt your worth and lose the confidence to show up authentically. You wonder when the other shoe will drop.

 **Be the Comforter:** You are great at comforting others first—even at the expense of your own comfort. Setting clear boundaries that don't become barriers or bunkers for your desires and needs is always a fraught process. You give much of yourself to many. You tend to overstay in relationships that don't serve you. "Don't rock the boat" is a strong mantra. Your Good Girl voice tells you that it is selfish to be self-centered and that humility and strength don't mix. You are scared to be alone because you were taught that being alone is bad. You long for someone to comfort you.

Not Enough: You have a crazy roommate in your head who is constantly telling you that you are not enough and that others are better, more valuable, more articulate, more likable, more beautiful, more qualified,  more deserving, more senior, more privileged, or younger than you. You stay in jobs that undervalue your talents. These stories keep you off center stage, and in some cultures, backstage. You stay in relationships that don't serve you so that you are not alone. You wonder what your purpose is.

 **Not Allowed:** You have not been given the option to experiment and spread your wings to see what is possible. It wasn't safe. You have dreamt big and played small. This might have happened first in your family

or culture of origin. Or it could be the unwritten rules of the game at work. In any case, you look out on a limited horizon and tread softly.

No matter where you find yourself on this spectrum at any point in time, these are all stories that shape our choices, well-being, and sense of self. However, they are just stories, meaning they are FICTION. They are not reality. They are only real if we allow them to be. This is where our agency to be epic comes in. We have the power to tell a different story.

Memories and beliefs are rear view mirrors that shape the stories we believe and tell *about* our lives and relationships. One of the unique traits of *Homo sapiens* is that we are amazing storytellers. Unlike other "*Homo*" species, the large brains of the *Homo sapiens* allow for the creation of "fictive language"—the ability to imagine and speak a narrative that is a "made up" theory of reality. Throughout the last 5,000 years, since the gods overthrew the goddesses, women have been cast as minor characters in the stories and myths authored by men. We have been portrayed with character flaws that have distorted our power and shaped the plot in a predictable direction. The result is that, even now, women are expected to fit into narrow archetypes along a spectrum of usual suspects: femme fatale, spinster, damsel in distress, seducer, evil stepmother, martyr, saint, witch, and more contemporarily, bitch. What do they have in common? These archetypes are more about men's desires, fears, and anxieties about women than they are a true reflection of women by women.

It is time for women to say "no" to having their character and plot defined by other storytellers and traditional storylines. Joseph Campbell, one of the greatest students of the myths that shape all storylines, is known for illuminating the overarching epic of the Hero's Journey, found in all cultures throughout recorded time, in his seminal book *The Hero with a Thousand Faces*. The "Hero" archetype is how we expect our leaders to look and behave when they are out and about in the world, slaying proverbial dragons and saving humanity. Women are longing to shift the plot, reimagine the characters, and reshape the story. Our "heroine" experiences the suit of armor as too tight, the horse too fast, the weapons too sharp, the princess too needy, the king too demanding, and the dragon misunderstood.

> "I shifted my story from living as a prisoner of lies into living as a Four-Star General of Truth."
> —MARCY, DECADE GAME CLASS OF 2020

I know that we women are longing to be heroines of our own story. We are ready to break the pattern set by the patriarchy for thousands of years. We yearn to embrace a different story that unleashes our unique talents and dreams. We long to step into our full power—body, intellect, and spirit—and be connected to our unique purpose—personally, professionally, philanthropically. We are eager to shape-shift from the "If Only" mindset that holds us back to the "Imagine If" field of possibilities that allow us to soar. And we want answers to these questions.

- When did I start playing small even though I was dreaming big?
- When did I start believing I wasn't magical?
- When did I forget that I am blessed with God-given talents?
- When did epic become out of reach?
- What is my purpose?
- How do I show up as my best self for me, the people I love, and the people who count on me?
- What is my genius?
- How do I recover my power?
- What would I do if I wasn't afraid?
- How do I gain clarity, confidence, and courage to design and live the best decade of my life so far?

Not only do we need answers, but the future is counting on us to find our truth. The earth, our societies, and our institutions are crying out for the rebalancing of feminine and masculine heroic energies so that empathy, insight, nurture, collaboration, compassion, and gratitude can combine with logic, reason, technology, and might to build a world that works for everyone. In other words, heroes and heroines alike are being called upon by future generations to step into the epic chapter of our lives to be the ancestors of an age to come—so that future generations can flourish and thrive.

I have been blessed to walk this journey of discovery with so many remarkable women, starting with my decade of teaching at Columbia. I wish you could meet every one of them so that they could inspire you the way they have inspired me. My experience with my students gave me a breathtaking insight. Women can't do this work of choosing to be epic on their own. My goodness, we have been trying to for decades. One step forward, three-quarters of a step back, over and over. It's exhausting, and over time, compromise, appeasement, and downsizing of dreams begin to feel like a groove instead of a rut.

This healing work needs to be done in a group where we can see both the tears of grief and exultation in each other's eyes. This insight propelled me to create subsequent cohorts of women to guide them through designing their custom-made lives through the eight-week Decade Game Master Class experience, or a longer program, The Remarkable Women's Journey, which I co-lead with the inimitable Lynne Twist and her amazing colleague Sara Vetter. Both programs attract women between the ages of thirty and seventy-five who are transitioning from one stage to another—having a family, searching for clarity and purpose in their career, shifting life "majors," moving from the "performance stage" to their "presence era," managing through family ruptures, seeking lost joy, trying to get "unstuck." As it turns out, regardless of where we are on life's path, our stories are similar. Our trials and triumphs are themes and variations of the same journey toward our essential selves—powerful, beautiful, committed, creative, epic souls.

You are not playing this game alone. Let me introduce you to just a few of the other players.

Meet twin sisters Priya and Ojaswini, who attended the Decade Game Master Class at different times. Born in India several minutes apart (Priya is older!), they both aggressively pursued degrees in engineering and business and careers at multinational companies while balancing the conservative nature of gender roles that is part of their culture. They are in the early chapters of learning to weave together the tapestry of their marriages and careers. They are keen to reconcile, for themselves, the cultural expectations they inherit with their own authentic relationship to power and ambition.

Some of you might relate to Lisa, a vivacious, athletic, "can-do," caring leader. When I met Lisa, she was the chief operating officer of a division of a major global bank. Lisa has more energy than almost anyone I know. That energy and her loving heart spilled over in many directions. She had recently taken on the responsibility of diversity, equity, and inclusion in her division. Lisa was the go-to mentor to a wide circle of men and women in her company, which just added to the expanding universe of friends that sought out her counsel. But Lisa was antsy and unsettled. Divorced after a short marriage, she was finding the work itself was not that meaningful. It didn't fill her heart. Given her entrepreneurial spirit, the pace of change in a large institution did not jive with her metabolic energy of "just go." She felt more and more caged in and wanted to spread her wings and create her own business that matched her greatest intentions and charged her spirit.

Your life right now might look more like Janice's. Her professional career was interrupted by severe grief due to unexpected illnesses and deaths in her immediate family—her father, mother, grandmother, and, finally, her beloved sister. After a decade of Mourner-in-Chief, it was time to re-engage with the world. But Janice didn't want to pick up where she left off. As a Black woman who was educated in mostly white Ivy League schools and had worked in an international company that skewed white in leadership, products, and customers, Janice was looking to re-enter as her most authentic, whole self.

Meet Tina, formerly a successful model, currently a world traveler, brilliant therapist, and one of the kindest people I know. From the outside in, it would be easy to assume that Tina feels complete in her life. From the inside out, with her therapist expertise, she knew there could be so much more. About to be remarried, she wanted to up her game both personally and professionally and be more proactive with the blessings she had been given. Having grown up dyslexic, her inside voice kept telling her that she didn't have the innate intelligence to make an exponential difference in her field. She was on a quest to supercharge her desire to take her clients to an entirely new level of self-development while, at the same time, working every day to be the best person she could be.

Maybe your Decade Game will look like Mary's. She retired in her mid-fifties after a spectacular career on Wall Street, where she was the global technology officer of a major investment bank. A divorced mother raising her daughter, Mary always found time during her big corporate job to volunteer with her church and other nonprofit organizations focusing on social justice, literacy, and the environment. She was motivated by the deep-held commitment that "every person should have the opportunity to experience inclusive, thriving, vibrant communities of caring and connectedness so that they are filled by the richness of a life that can transform." In creating the next chapter of her life, Mary wanted to be as fully engaged as she had previously been. Now that she had all the time in the world to focus, she was looking for clarity on a pathway that would fill her up to the level of her talents and dreams.

Perhaps you're more like Cheryl. Quiet and unassuming, she has been inspired by big ideas and people committed to making a difference in the world. She played behind the scenes working tirelessly to support NGO leaders who set out to change the world. As the executive assistant to the president of The Hunger Project, she traveled throughout India and Africa, where she saw firsthand the devastating effects of poverty, hunger, and malnutrition. Then, as one of the 1.6 million people in 2016 who heard "you have cancer," Cheryl focused full-time on applying her knowledge of nutritional modalities to healing her cancer. Concurrently, she tackled her emotional stress head-on, finally pursuing a divorce that was long in the making as well as doing healing work with her son. With her cancer in remission and her divorce almost final, Cheryl was ready for a decade journey of discovery.

Stephene told me it was time for her. She had recently moved her beloved spouse of many years into a small family-focused memory care home for people living with Alzheimer's disease. She had enjoyed an amazing career on the national stage, even running for Congress. She raised four kids plus three stepchildren. However, in the last several years, her life was reduced to being a caregiver for her spouse and widowed father. "I know I can do amazing things; I have done amazing things. I still have trouble with doing for myself. Doing for myself continues to feel selfish and not 'what a Good Girl' does." Even though she had been an adventurous and inveterate traveler most of her life, her field of vision had become local. Stephene was ready to live again. "I should live the next decade and longer, living in my story, not someone else's."

You might relate to any of these women or a little part of each of them. As we go on, you will see how they have played the Decade Game, but now it's time for you to start playing, so get comfortable and open your mind and heart. Let the next few paragraphs take you on an imaginal journey into the future. Are you ready? Here we go:

It is ten years from today, how old are you now? You've just had one of the greatest days of your life. Everything you've experienced today epitomizes all that you have worked toward and all that you've contributed to the universe—to your own inner world, to your vocation, to your family, friends, and loved ones. You feel an incredible sense of satisfaction and accomplishment for all the experiences, knowledge, and relationships that you have intentionally built over the last ten years that have culminated in your ability to have the kind of day you just had. As you (choose a beloved end-of-day activity—a quiet, contemplative moment, a glass of wine, a walk on the beach—your choice! This is YOUR game!), you take a moment to reflect on the last decade. You are delighted. The choices you have made on where to invest your time, trust, treasures, and talents have brought you to this place of centeredness, peace, and impact. Your relationship with your faith, friends, and family has deepened in amazing and surprising ways. Your impact in your community is palpable. Your accomplishments, big and small, are inspirational.

How will you describe that day? What happened? Who were you with? Who reached out to you? How did you feel? How did they feel? What impact did you make on others? How many "separate" threads seemed to come together into the tapestry you had dreamed of ten years ago?

Are you dreaming? Good. Dream a little more. And when you're ready, I want you to write a journal entry dated ten years into the future. Let's say 500 to 600 words. Not too long but full of details of this extraordinary dream day. Be bold! And think EPIC! This future day needs to be a day that would need a decade of meaningful choices, experiences, knowledge, and relationships to achieve. It should not be a day that could realistically happen in a shorter time frame. (Now, put that journal entry away until you have finished this book. At the end of this book, I will invite you to pull it out again to see what more your future self wants to say.)

Playing the Decade Game allows you to design your own game board, define what winning looks and feels like, and create all your own rules. Every great game has a page-turning narrative arc, interactivity, compelling choices, exciting surprises—and is fun to play over and over again. Women are ready to play their best game so that their life reads like an epic.

Rules of the Game:
If you are not having fun, you are playing someone else's game.

Section II

Choose to Be Epic

A Splendid Torch

"This is the true joy in life, the being used for a purpose recognized by yourself as a mighty one; the being a force of nature instead of a feverish, elfish little clod of ailments and grievances complaining that the world will not devote itself to making you happy.

"I am of the opinion that my life belongs to the whole community, and as long as I live it is my privilege to do for it whatever I can. I want to be thoroughly used up when I die, for the harder I work the more I live. I rejoice in life for its own sake. Life is no 'brief candle' for me. It is a sort of splendid torch which I have got hold of for the moment, and I want to make it burn as brightly as possible before handing it on to future generations."

—GEORGE BERNARD SHAW, an advocate of equal rights and a healthy lifestyle, and the playwright of *Pygmalion*, the story of the transformation of a woman

Chapter 3

Power Plays on Purpose

Here is an ironic paradox. In my conversations with women around the world, they are 100 percent committed to empowering others—yet they are squeamish about the idea of intentionally seeking to become as powerful as possible, let alone admit a desire to be "epic." Before we can even entertain the idea of epic, women need to get comfortable with the notion of power. *Power is just a current.* Like electricity or water, it's just a force that is neither good nor evil. It is used to shift something forward, backward, up or down, faster or slower. This power current comes in many forms or currencies: knowledge, relationships, status, personality, resources, and beauty, none of which, on their own, are positive or negative. The prepositions that join up with power are equally neutral—power over, power against, power on behalf of, power for. It is a person's intention and purpose that directs the power, creates the outcomes, and holds all the meaning.

I understand women's aversion to power. First, they are rejecting the way they have seen power used in the past and, thus, are attributing adverse connotations to power. Second, when women seek to be powerful, the reaction to them by both men and women is ambivalent and, at times, even antagonistic. Third, there are scant role models for women to show how to wear power gracefully, graciously, and generously. Trying to walk that narrow balance beam has left many women bruised from their falls. Finally, being intentional about getting power doesn't feel feminine or sexy. Instead, it conflicts with the intense psychological desire of women to be loved for their womanhood.

Now let's unpack epic. The Greek word "epic" was first used to describe long-form poems with heroic narratives depicting larger-than-life heroes doing great deeds. In our hearts, women long to tell an epic story of their own life: a story of love, service, contribution, courage, sacrifice, humanity, sensuality, sexuality, creation, accomplishments, adventure, and their own unique tales of "derring-do" (i.e., "daring to do"). More often, given the Good Girls that we are, we tell this story to ourselves—but to no one else. False modesty has been bred into our bones so deeply that we become the unindicted co-conspirators of our "smallness." Our journey into epic begins when we remember that we are all guilty of this, yet none of us are to blame. Rather, this is the effect of eons of the patriarchic conditioning that has confined us to this version of the script.

Here is the news you can use. EPIC! is a choice. I am not talking about the current "masculine" hierarchical construct of "epic" that tends to imply greater than, larger than, richer than, closer to the top, "master of the universe" kind of epic. I am using this in a relational "feminine" construct of getting closer to the center of what is most essential. Without us, life doesn't happen. We create life. We also have a choice to create a life that is worth dying for every day. I know this is hard to visualize. Women need to erase the "win at all costs" image that immediately comes to mind. We also must fight through the Good Girl conditioning of "Who, me?"

I have found it helpful to conjure up a different feeling to describe the way you are with yourself and others when you are in flow and embodying your best self. I ask women to create their own acronym for EPIC! that allows them to name the energies and emotional outcomes that illustrate their best being and doing. What would your EPIC! acronym be?

E	P	I	C
Essence	Presence	Inspired	Courage
Empathy	Power	Illustrious	Compassion
Evolution	Profound	Illuminated	Creation
Exalted	Possibilities	Intention	Charisma
Extraordinary	Prosperity	Impact	Celebration
Emergent	Proud	Impressive	Classic
Embodied	Purpose	Innovative	Clarity
Embracing	Practice	Integrity	Committed
?	?	?	?

Epic is a choice you can make today so that you can create a life by your own design and desires and not default to old plot lines and downtrodden characters. Although EPIC! is about connecting to your essential being, it is not passive. You will need to work at finding and embodying this truth. Here are some of the power plays embedded in the Decade Game that will ignite your epic-ness.

Powering Up Your Story

You are your best-kept secret—and only you know the real story. You are totally enough. Once we shake ourselves free of the negative stories we've adopted or adapted to, we can begin to make the power of story work for us. One of the gifts that separates us from other sentient beings is our love for and fluency in storytelling. Our origin stories found in all religions and faiths have given mankind the ultimate meaning for millennia. The stories we tell ourselves give us our own meaning. Every day and every choice provide us with the opening to ask, "Is this a story that serves me?" The Decade Game starts by defining your epic quest with your personal origin story and framing the answers to the following questions:

- Why am I on the planet?
- What is my overarching purpose?
- If not me, then who?
- What is the meta-story that allows me to discover meaning for myself every day and create meaning for others?
- What story is worth dying for?
- What will the future generations remember me for?
- What is my unique contribution to a world that works?

Powering up your story gives you permission to set aside both self-betrayal and false modesty and let your epic truth unfold.

Powering Up Your Imagination

If you can imagine and envision it, you are it. With our growing understanding of neuroplasticity, we have a greater appreciation for how visualization reprograms the brain to be open to new possibilities and the confidence that they are attainable. Research shows that the daily practice of visualizing your dreams as already complete can rapidly accelerate your achievement of those dreams, goals, and ambitions. Dreaming our biggest dreams—and then believing they can happen—is the game of life, well played.

Think about the magic of a jigsaw puzzle. We choose the puzzle based on the picture on the front of the box—one that lights us up, inspires us, and invites us into the imaginal adventure, with the confidence that every piece we need is already inside the box. Like a jigsaw puzzle, every single piece we need for this to be the best decade of our lives is already within us. Dollar rich or dollar poor, we have every asset, talent, treasure, and previous experience necessary to have a life of meaning and purpose. We need to keep the image on the jigsaw box in front of us to guide our choices. Even when we are sure that pieces must be missing, we know in our hearts that we have what it takes. We are ready to take on the adventure of puzzling through to get the pieces to fit exactly right.

Powering Up Your Ambition

I have already noted that ambition is a "dirty" word for most women. Let's defang that right now. I am not talking about the type of ambition that feels like a bottomless pit: needing affirmation and approval from the outside-in to fuel our drive. That type of ambition is an imposter. It is exhausting and soul-crushing. I'm talking about authentic inside-out ambition that brings sparkle to your quest to fulfill your dreams. Think about ambition as your life force, your desire to grow. Your mission on this earth demands that you know how to nurture and tend it. To do this, you need to play both offense and defense, encouraging the longing to accomplish inside of you and sending the "Good Girl" to her room for a time-out when she tries to hold you back. This requires total vigilance to keep your ambition fired up. It is dependent on other "naughty" words that also have a terrible reputation for women yet are essential to play the Decade Game—mastery and recognition.

My thinking on this has been helped immensely by the work of the brilliant New York–based psychiatrist Anna Fels in her ground-breaking work *Necessary Dreams: Ambition in Women's Changing Lives.* Fels argues that ambition is a function of mastery and recognition. It is a sensitive simultaneous equation where ambition can be easily downsized if building mastery is halted and/or recognition for one's mastery is mixed or negative, either by you or others. I am not talking about recognition as an incessant need for approval to counter-act the "not enough-ness" voice inside. I am referring to the recognition and appreciation of our sufficiency.

Recognition, Fels writes, is something that makes us better at what we do, and without it, ambitions die. Without positive recognition, most women pull back from their commitment to mastery.

Let's examine this equation.

Ambition: This is the desire to accomplish, which is at the root of all human beings' ability to develop. It is easy for those of you with children, or who can remember being a child, to conjure up the somatic memory triggered by these words, "Mommy. Daddy. Look at me. Look what I can do." The urge to accomplish is the essential growth hormone that triggers movement: physical, spiritual, emotional, and intellectual. Without this impetus, it would be next to impossible to get off Mommy and Daddy's lap and venture out into the world to create your own self.

Mastery: This is the objective, the end state, of your desire to accomplish. Knowing what mastery looks like and having role models that manifest that vision is the gateway to the future. It's like selecting your major in college. After reading the catalog describing the required and elective courses, you begin to imagine yourself already successful in a chosen field. You are then in the best position to choose the experiences, knowledge, skills, and teachers that will make up the best curriculum. In the Decade Game, the pursuit of mastery is not just about your goals of "doing." Doing does not equal mastery. The epic quest involves your commitment to mastery in the field of being. Mastery is not about achieving the zenith—rather, it is discovering the essence, the center of your unique artistry, brilliance, and integrity. Much of the "juice" in life, the epic-ness and rapture of being alive, comes from a commitment to move from "good enough" to striving for great.

Recognition: This means to be known for something. Recognition is a mirror on the wall in an often chaotic world telling you that you are on track. It's like a compass guiding you to let you know, "a little further to the left, turn three degrees to the south." Recognition, literally "to be examined and known anew," lets you know that you are seen, gotten, and appreciated. The pursuit of recognition differs from the neediness, which stems from the "I am not worthy" story. It is not the obsession with exceptionalism that pervades our consumer culture. Growing in mastery increases your own clarity of your own self-worth and provides the stimulus to be validated and encouraged by others. Positive recognition for who you are and who you are working to become is a form of giving and receiving love. It is a way for someone to express admiration for you. Admiration means to regard someone with wonder, to marvel at the miracle of that human being— her struggles, her resilience, her grace, her commitment, the quality of her presence, and yes, how all that brilliance translates into the genius of her doing. The added miracle is that positive recognition works for both the giver and receiver. Research has proven that positive recognition triggers happy hormones—dopamine, serotonin, oxytocin—in both the appreciator and the appreciated. This links directly to mastery because the one who is appreciated appreciates. Negative recognition (which is different from constructive feedback) is a form of judgment and has the opposite effect of deflating ambition.

Take a moment to let this sink in by considering these questions:

- What are your greatest ambitions—at home, at work, and in the world?
- When have you downsized your ambitions? Why did you do so?
- When do you give your power away? How does that make you feel?
- Where in your life have you settled for "good enough?"

Women have been playing not to lose for centuries because of their allergic reaction to all these naughty words: power, ambition, mastery, and recognition. These words have combined in cultural, political, and emotional ways to create a vicious cycle that limited the fuel of our becoming. "Honey, aren't you shooting too high?" "I don't know how you do it! Being a mother and traveling so much for work." "Do you think you are really ready?" "It would be better if…" The more negative recognition, or self-talk, we get for our dreams, the more we have downsized our horizons of what was possible, and ambition falls. The more ambition falls, confidence drops, and mastery recedes. All a downward spiral.

Here is the great news. You can control this equation yourself and regulate the power of your ambition. Instead of letting the vicious Goldilocks cycle have the world judge you for being "too this or too that," you can become the source of your own virtuous circle of growing your brilliance in all areas of your life. This starts when you recognize and celebrate your own accomplishments and seek out recognition from others. How can you start this transformational flywheel? Volunteer for a committee, join a women's group, start your own group, let others know about your accomplishments and aspirations, ask for feedback. *You are then set up to play to win.*

Think about the games you have bought and played repeatedly in your life. If you are my age, you remember the board games Monopoly, Life, Risk, Careers—or for those born after 1980, maybe you are thinking about the video games of Zelda, Super Mario Brothers, Star Craft, Sim City, or World of Warcraft. You buy a game for its epic objective—a quest that is exciting, bold, and requires your utmost focus and attention. With the power plays of story, imagination, and ambition, you are ready to begin to power up your purpose, your epic quest.

Powering Up Your Purpose

Why are you on the planet? Most people I know are not sure of the answer to this—even though it is one of the most important questions you will ever ask yourself. The more targeted and precise your answer, the more majestic your life will feel. The good news is that you have a purpose, whether you know it or not. Throughout your life, there has been an underlying theme or melodic song line in many of the experiences, decisions, and adventures that have meant the most. Getting clear on purpose is hard for women because there are so many contenders. Given women's multiple priorities and commitments—at home, at work, in the community—it's difficult to find the beacon that illuminates our path for all decisions.

Here is a definition that will help you get clear on your purpose. ***Purpose is your own theory of change about how the world gets better, in a way that you believe you can make a unique contribution.*** You most likely share that theory of change with many others—to make the world healthier, or smarter, or more loving, or more forgiving, or more sustainable, or more just, or more courageous. Your purpose is where you feel called to contribute for your own unique reasons, attributes, qualities, and background. And contrary to your false modesty peeking out again from behind the page, you do have a unique contribution to make. As I mentioned earlier, there is no person in the history of this planet that can exactly equal your way of doing, your perspective in how you see the world, and the truth you can voice.

Your purpose is not a "point of view" that could change over time. Nor is purpose a description of "how" you might plan to contribute at any point in time. Think about purpose as a "Stand" that is incontrovertible, universal, and lasts throughout your lifetime and beyond. It is your raison d'être that is waiting to be discovered.

I learned about the power of taking a Stand from Lynne Twist, my teacher, friend, and colleague. Lynne is a recognized global visionary committed to alleviating poverty, ending world hunger, and supporting social justice and environmental sustainability. From working with Mother Teresa in Calcutta to the refugee camps in Ethiopia to the threatened rainforests of the Amazon, as well as guiding the philanthropy of some of the world's wealthiest families and advising the women who have won the Nobel Peace Prize, Lynne's breadth of knowledge and experience has led her to profound insights about the social tapestry of the world and the historical landscape of these current times.

She describes the attributes of a Stand this way:

- A Stand transcends all positions.
- Taking your Stand allows you to let go of positions.
- A Stand has the capacity to move the world because it honors the usefulness of all positions.
- Who you are is where you Stand.
- Your Stand cannot be accomplished in your lifetime.
- Your Stand doesn't have specific goals or metrics.
- In your Stand, you join the Stand-holders of history.
- Your Stand is available to anyone.
- Your Stand gives meaning to everything you are doing.

You have the recipe for an epic life when your life's journey is always in service of your Stand. Here are some tips to get clear on your Stand.

Your Stand is like an organization's vision, which they share with other similar organizations. Think about it like this. You are the CEO of "You.Org," and you share your purpose with other CEOs in the same nonprofit sector—i.e., improving health, empowering women, advancing social justice, stewarding climate change, promoting faith, appreciating the healing powers of art. Your Stand is the cause that most calls to your heart and motivates you to contribute your best self. You will contribute to that vision in your own unique way—and that becomes the personal mission of You.Org.

Don't think you need to invent a unique cause or purpose, or dig deep within yourself. You are born into a world of causes, which existed before you were born and will be there after you die. You will find your purpose already lives inside you as you reflect on the causes that have gripped you over the years, the stories that have broken your heart, and the ones that inspired you to give greatly of yourself. I have found that my Stand reflects the growing awareness I have personally experienced on how the world could be more fair, more safe, or more just.

I began to think about my purpose at age eight during the election of JFK in 1960 when I decided to answer his call of what I could do for my country. We were in the middle of the Cold War with the Soviet Union, and I was experiencing atomic bomb drills where they told us to hide in our school lockers. My other vivid memory was my mother deciding that we couldn't drink fresh milk due to fear of atomic fallout on the grass that the cows ate. (To this day, my stomach turns over every time I recall the smell of the horrid powdered milk we had to drink!) JFK, a profile in courage, called on all Americans to wake up not just to the threat of war but the possibilities of greatness and personal responsibility. The theory of change that began to emerge for me was the importance of courageous leaders to champion a world that works for everyone.

This was consistent with what I was observing with my inspiring mother, Minna Buck. My mother was one of only two women in her law school class at the University of Chicago in the 1940s. Growing up, my mother championed every program of President Johnson's Great Society in upstate New York. The War on Poverty, the Crusade for Opportunity—you name it, she did it. I saw the positive impact she made on so many undersupported families, particularly women, as she worked tirelessly in their service. I also experienced the effect of her choices on me. I, along with my two siblings who were one year older and younger than me, respectively, was envied by everyone else in our school. My mom was the only mother in my elementary school who worked outside of the home, so we didn't stay at school for lunch. No lunchroom or supervisor—instead, we got to walk by ourselves, hand in hand, every day to a nearby diner for lunch. Sitting on the lunch counter stools like three jelly beans, we were able to have a hamburger, cherry phosphate, and a donut for lunch, all for thirty-five cents. What joy! What freedom!

Watching my mom, I knew that my Stand was related to improving the world for women and their families. Your purpose can shift over the years. It gets more sophisticated in the way you describe your theory of change and why it calls to you, but it is in there somewhere. Today, my theory of change still resonates with my early ideas that leaders matter and empowering women matters. Many of our institutions—healthcare, education, politics, business—are no longer serving humanity and will require courageous leaders to take the hero/heroine's journey to champion a better future. Today, I Stand for and with heart-based, courageous leaders who can find their magic, trust their magic, and use their magic with honor to create goodness for others.

Your Stand is the song line, the epic poem, your north star that runs through your decisions and choices. It is not something that will ever be achieved in your lifetime. It's humanity's quest and your **Life's Work.**

I know the question of why you are here is scary to answer because it feels so "life and death" and consequential. What I find fascinating is how easy it is to come up with a good first pass at your Stand. In a recent Decade Game Master Class, a group of amazing women came up with the first draft of their Stand after reflecting on it overnight. These Stands are amazingly simple yet universal. If they seem like clichés, they are. Clichés get a bad name, but, at their essence, they are a truism. They reflect the answers to these questions:

- Why are you on the planet?
- What is your Life's Work?
- What "cause" fires you up and brings tears to your eyes?
- What conditions in the world today break your heart?
- What change in the world would you like to see?
- Where do people count on you for help?
- How would a loved one describe the reason you were put on this earth?

As you read them, note how our Decade Gamers' Stands resonate with their choices to date, heartbreaks they have experienced, and their own core wounds that they have spent their life healing. Their Stands complete the sentence, "I Stand for a world where…"

- From Fran who has spent her career championing environment integrity in a region of the US: *the preservation of the beauty and mystery of Nature invites people to live fully in its embrace.*
- From Priya—our young software engineer: *people are seen and supported for their truest potential.*
- From Laura—a gospel singer in her earlier career, then music producer who has fought throughout her life to be seen and heard: *voice comes back to the voiceless, and all voices are heard and honored.*
- From Lori—a university professor teaching organizational design: *the power of innovation changes lives.*
- From Amy—an artist and sculptor working on civic projects: *creativity abounds so that new models can ensure we have a world that works for everyone.*
- Juliana—a veterinarian: *the voiceless—i.e., animals, disenfranchised people, the environment—are heard and honored.*
- Patty—a healthcare industry executive: *everyone has access and agency for healthy choices.*
- Susan—senior executive in financial services with a focus on entrepreneurs and women-owned businesses: *everyone trusts in their own value and potential and finds joy in their path.*

- Anh—émigré from Vietnam, young mother, and real estate consultant: *every girl (and boy) can stand in their full power since birth.*
- June—personal and spiritual development coach and teacher: *sacred and beloved community is available to all sentient beings.*
- Tina—our therapist specializing in the elderly and women with cancer: *every human being can be proud of "who I am" and help others be proud of "who they are."*
- Lisa—our executive turned entrepreneur: *no one is alone or left behind (and that all people can realize there are no limits to what is possible).*

"People say that what we're all seeking is a meaning for life. I don't think that's what we're really seeking. I think that what we're seeking is an experience of being alive, so that our life experiences on the purely physical plane will have resonances with our own innermost being and reality, so that we actually feel the rapture of being alive."

—JOSEPH CAMPBELL, *THE POWER OF MYTH*

Your Stand informs, guides, and shapes your everyday decisions and actions. No matter what you are doing—interacting with a loved one, meditating, making decisions on the job, or choosing to make a philanthropic gift—your Stand serves as your compass, allowing you to discover meaning for yourself in the everyday and create meaning for others by your commitment. Now it is time to do your first draft. Taking guidance from the Stands you read above, think about your hopes of how the world could become better that calls you to offer your unique contribution to that epic outcome and complete the sentence that starts, "I Stand for a world where..."

It is a work in progress to name such a big thing as your life's purpose. Remember that iteration is the key to design. Research shows that iterating your initial idea seven times leads to 1,000 percent better outcome. Here is key design guidance for your Stand:

- No wrong answers.
- Keep the "I" and the "how" out of your Stand. The rest of the Decade Game board will handle that.
- Don't worry that you don't know yet what this means for you. Just speak from your heart.
- Use evocative keywords that inspire you.
- What is the most inspiring way to say this that addresses a transformational shift in the world that you are deeply passionate about?
- Can you see this as a compass for all areas of your life—personal, professional, communal?
- Make it compelling, not complex.

Rules of the Game:
If you are not part of the problem,
you can't be part of the solution.

Chapter 4

The Power of Claiming Your Destiny

Think about your favorite characters, the heroes and heroines from childhood to the present, who have inspired your life. What makes a character "epic"? They have a distinct identity that illuminates their "one-of-a-kind-ness." They are known and named by others for what makes them unique. Their superpowers are on display. Their being and actions are a manifestation of their Stand and reflect the character of their character.

For my therapist friend Tina, her favorite character is Joan of Arc. This character always calls her to lean into her

Stand: *"being proud of 'who I am' and helping others be proud of 'who they are.'"*

For our "recovering corporate executive," Lisa, who is building her own business, her favorite idol these days is Brené Brown. This is consistent with Lisa's Stand: *"I stand for enabling connections so that nobody is alone or left behind."*

Here is another aspect of superheroes. These characters are activated by a sense of destiny, encouraged to defy boundaries, and focused on a win that is bigger than themselves. Being and doing EPIC! is all about the journey. However, like in any game, you need to have a clear view of what winning looks like to plan your next best moves. This idea was best captured by a wonderful quote from the great comedienne Lily Tomlin, who said, "I always knew I wanted to be someone—I just didn't realize I needed to be more specific."

In the last chapter, we focused on your overarching Stand that is your life's work. In this chapter, you will learn how to name your avatar—your imaginal superheroine—and claim your decade destiny.

The Story So Far

A common concept in history across religions, cultures, and time is that knowing the name of something or someone gives one power over that thing or person. A commonly cited example from Genesis is when God said, "Let there be light," and there was light, followed by God giving Man the right to name all animals and to have dominion over them. Naming something brings it into existence and gives it a life force.

The intangible becomes tangible. The impossible becomes possible. Amorphous ideas find form and become goals and definitions of success.

I see this all the time in my corporate strategic consulting, executive coaching, and my own spiritual work. Naming the real work and defining what success could look and feel like creates a dynamic that can no longer be ignored. Hope turns into action. The genie is out of the bottle.

The power of naming reframes the way we think and feel about any challenge or situation. Naming our identity and what we long for also changes the way other people see and perceive us. Before we can start building the future, we must make sure we are entering the game with our truest identity unpolluted by any of the old names or stories that we assigned ourselves (or had assigned for us) that are no longer functional. We want to start the Decade Game from the perspective of our Superwoman persona, not her alter ego.

There are a lot of old stories and names to shake off. As our minds take us down memory lane, it is like looking at pictures at an exhibition depicting our traumas and triumphs, our highs and our lows. Each picture stands alone, a snapshot that created emotional impact, either positive or negative. We don't think about the result of the moving picture. My experience is that the pictures of our failures and missteps, combined with the cumulative experience of the Goldilocks syndrome of never "just right," begin to color our memory and diminish the trajectory of our flight path.

Exercise: The Story So Far

Here is the exercise they did. You can follow along and do it, too.

Tell me the story of your life so far by drawing a dot on the timeline and noting, with headlines, the five most important triumphs (rated six and above, with ten your highest point) and the five biggest disasters/disappointments (rated five to one, with one your lowest point). Include personal and/or professional events that have had a significant impact on you, your confidence, and your sense of self.

When you finish charting your history, look at the trajectory that has gotten you to where you are today. Standing in the present and looking back, if you were going to write the story of that journey, taking into account the triumphs and the trials, what would be the Title and Subtitle of the Book? As an example, look at the graph from one of our participants.

EXAMPLE:

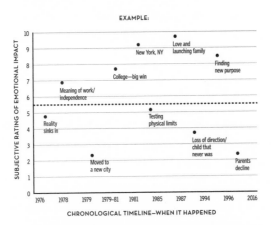

MY HEART'S JOURNEY: The Journey of a Resilient Woman Towards Wholeness

You can't design a fabulous decade if you enter it burdened by the baggage of the past. A critical starting point in your design is to re-cast your character with the best plotline. In the fall of 2020, a very challenging year indeed, I led a Decade Game Master Class virtually for eight weeks for thirty-two amazing, talented women ranging in ages from thirty-four to seventy. At the start of the Master Class, the participants carried on their faces the stress and strain of a year of pandemic, politics, and societal perturbation and its attendant personal, professional, and public uncertainty. We needed to do some level-setting for a strong start. Each class member needed to pick up her character, brush her off, and name her story so far.

Our participants did this exercise in the first session and emerged joyous and excited about what the future might hold. They were lit up based on their realization of how resilient, strong, and courageous they were. Listen to the power of agency, hope, and self-forgiveness that echoes in the titles and subtitles of their story so far:

- *The Girl Who Put Her Head Down and Got It Done: What's Ahead for the Next Third?*
- *Girl Without Baggage: The story of a strong woman constantly working toward self-freedom*
- *Full Circle: Or how I lost my oomph*
- *NY Girl Goes Global: Peaks & Valleys & the ups and downs of the same experience*
- *Bonnie from Iowa: Taking the Scenic Route Home to Myself*

- *Finding My Truth: The journey of a young woman loving to learn and learning to love*
- *Thinking Outside the Box: Why Doesn't She Just Try to Fit In?*
- *Blood Diamond: The Becoming Journey of a Fighter*
- *Unexpected Strength: When the first thing happens to you, could be the best thing*
- *The Tale of the Unexpected Journey: Distractions, adventures, lack of confidence, and hope*
- *Flying the Coop to Nest Within: A small-town girl seeks adventure beyond borders to find her way to grow roots at home and within*
- *My Epic Nomadic Journey: Imagining my north star on my next horizon*
- *Resilience: Never an obstacle I couldn't beat (book 1)*
- *On the Road to Joy: Always Going Deeper*
- *Finding My Truth in Love and Work: Not the destination, but the path*
- *Phoenix Rising from the Ashes: MY TIME NOW*
- *Walking in the World: The story of me; looking back, looking forward*
- *Chameleon No More: Time to stitch my own coat of many colors*
- *Great Highs and Great Lows: The many places I've been: Relentless pursuit of bringing new futures into reality*
- *The Don't Look Back Tour: You Got This*
- *Unfinished Pursuits of My Heart: Thriving with imperfections*
- *Where Do I Fit?: I'm making my time—my way*
- *Go Ahead, Throw A Curve Ball: I'll catch it*

- *My Wild and Wonderful Wander: Owning & Defining My Wanderlust*
- *Healing a Broken Heart: A story of births, deaths, and being me*
- *The Resiliency Chronicles: Strength in all the broken places*

I think you can agree that these would be wonderful books to read. Do you see your story in some of them? By rewriting the story so far, you can reframe your history and reclaim the majesty and power of your character. Even if you were not born "sunny side up" as I was, but rather "butter-side down" (like my husband), the power of naming your true story so far is a Jiu-Jitsu move that reframes possibilities and perspectives.

The History of the Future

Having reclaimed the true story of your journey so far, you are ready to design what comes next. It's time to write the history of the future, your decade destination. This is the objective of the game—who will your character be a decade from now? What does winning look like for you? How to name your becoming? The challenge is to put it into words, in the boldest, most concise, descriptive way, how you will know yourself AND be known by the world as the truest expression of your greatest gifts and dreams come true.

The words destination and destiny come from the same root—*destinare*: to make firm that which has been established. These words conjure up a desired place in the future that we long for. To bring this future into reality will require your greatest talents of make-believe. If you can believe it, then you can make it happen. So, suspend all the antibodies that say "Yeah, but…" Without the filter of fear, resource constraints, push-backs, "what ifs," and false modesty, what could be your greatest destiny?

Human brains are funny things. We're not as smart as we think we are. We only see what we expect to see, what we have seen before. It seems like magic, but if we visualize something concretely enough, our brains begin to function as if we already did it—in real life! Athletic coaches have known this for years. That's why they're always telling their athletes to visualize the finish line. The perfect swing. Breaking the tape. The gold medal platform. Once you can see it and feel it in your body, your mind begins to open all kinds of new neural channels to make it happen. This metamorphosis isn't easy, given the gravitational pull of your current experience. It requires specificity and detail combined with desire and longing.

Let me give you an example of how this works. Linda had a stellar career so far, surprising for someone so young. Having studied political science and government in college, she envisioned a career in national security. After several jobs in communications in Washington, she landed a job as press secretary for the US Department of Veteran Affairs. Her energy, work ethic, and intellect caught the attention of the higher-ups, and she did a tour of duty in Afghanistan, serving as the senior communications expert supporting the work of the multinational operational headquarters in Kabul. When we met, Linda had transitioned into the private sector and was working for a global communications agency. It was meaningful work. It paid the bills. But it wasn't nourishing her soul or contributing to her Stand.

Like most people looking for meaning and purpose in their "job," Linda was beginning to look around. She wanted to get back into her first love—national security and public service. She was deep in inquiry. "What should my next step be?" In the Decade Game, that is the wrong question for three reasons.

- It locks you into a fixed mindset that the future needs to be a linear extension of the past.
- It diminishes the range of your future aspirations to better align with your past accomplishments.
- It shortens your time horizon and pushes you into a trap of compromising for the "probable" incremental win instead of shooting for the "impossible" exponential destination.

I reframed the question for her. "What has been your greatest dream ever about who you could become to have the coolest job in the world?" She knew it in an instant. "I have always wanted to be Secretary of the Army. I know I could be great at that job!" And why not? In a decade, she would be older than Barack Obama was when he was elected president. With that destination in mind, I saw her whole body relax. Instead of the uncertainty of what her next job should be, she had the clarity of what she wanted to learn and experience in whatever job she took as a stepping-stone toward possibilities.

There is a bigger transformation afoot when you name and claim your destiny. Did you have a chance to watch Amanda Gorman, the first American to be named National Youth Poet Laureate who captivated a nation during her dramatic reading of her poem "The Hill We Climb" at the 2021 inauguration of President Biden? In a television interview afterward on CNN, she brought tears of joy to anchorman Anderson Cooper when she declared that she planned to run for president one day. As soon as she said it, a miracle happened. Her relationship with herself and our relationship with her changed. She believed it, and we believed it. The heretofore impossible became possible. And the trajectory of her orbit shifted.

As I write this, Amanda has just signed a breakthrough contract with the Estée Lauder Company that is changing the face and raising the bar for celebrity endorsements. She will become the first Estée Lauder "Global Changemaker"—as opposed to just an ambassador or "face," pushing product. Her vision is to harness the power and promise of the market and moral forces to make a difference in the world. "I'm never just lending my body or my face," Ms. Gorman said. "They are getting my spirit, my breath, my brain." But, she said, "rather than letting the world tell me what I should be doing"—or not doing—"I realized this is my moment to tell the world what it needs to get done." As our youngest poet laureate, Amanda Gorman is introducing her epic form of poetic justice into the world.

> "If we could change ourselves, the tendencies in the world would also change. As a man changes his own nature, so does the attitude of the world change towards him."
>
> —MAHATMA GANDHI

Creating the Winning Strategy

Here is the big Decade Game secret. Your job is no longer what someone is paying you to do today. That's so last decade. Achieving your decade destination is now your full-time job. Once you name the epic character you would love to become, you are then responsible for saying "yes" to the experiences, knowledge, relationships, and actions to fully embody that future. When you sign up to design the best decade of your life, there is never time off or time out! You're always on the job, from the moment you get up to the moment you go to sleep. Your decade destination is your new **Job Description**.

Let's now translate that amazing decade journal entry you did in Chapter 2 into a compelling job description for our heroine. To do that, you need to be specific and evocative. Imagine that you are choosing an avatar of your most masterful self. This avatar speaks volumes about your dreams, knowledge, skills, and hopes in all aspects of your life. She is the declaration of who you are in your wildest dreams, having devoted a decade to become your most authentic, powerful self. This declaration also serves as a "choice architecture" guiding you to say "yes" to the right things and people—all in the right way.

The best form of a decade job description is a short title that illuminates your future rank, superpowers, and mandate. It should start with the words, "Wouldn't it be cool if I was known by myself, by the people who love me, and by the people who count on me as…" It should not be a traditional title, e.g., "I am a VP of compliance with the responsibility for making sure our product is safe for our customers." Your decade job description should be an iconic statement of the unique mission you have chosen to accept. Here is a hint. Imagine it on a calling card. You will know you are on track if it is both awesome and makes you giggle.

Exercise:
Name Your Decade Destination

It is time to play another game within the Decade Game. Do you remember playing Mad Libs as a kid? You would be given a sentence or story, and you would fill in the blanks in a way that would make the Mad Lib fun and outrageous. To create a powerful decade destination that captures the essence and excitement of your decade journal entry, you can follow this format:

"Wouldn't it be cool if ten years from now I was known by the people who love me, as well as those who count on me, as:

Exciting Adjective + *Powerful Subject* +
Dynamic Verb + <u>Targeted Object</u> +
EPIC OUTCOME

Here are a few examples of Decade Gamers' job descriptions, starting with my sixty to seventy game. At sixty, I was retiring from twenty years as a principal and management consultant for EY. Having been "corporate" for decades, I wanted my decade destination to be 1) age-appropriate and 2) in service to my Stand—*to help courageous leaders trust their magic and mobilize others for transformation.*

I also wanted to transition my relationship with ambition from showing up as the warrior/rock star to showing up as an elder. My "Mad Lib" decade destination at seventy is to be known as an Organizational *Shaman* **Encouraging** <u>Humans</u> TO LIVE EPIC LIVES.

Let's revisit some of the women you met in Chapter 2 to see their future identities.

Priya, our thirty-seven-year-old mother and software engineer, is growing in all aspects of her life. She stands for a world where people are seen and supported for their truest potential. Her decade destination for forty-seven is to be known as Courageous *Designer* **Facilitating** <u>Women's Paths</u> TO EPIC-NESS THROUGH SELF-DISCOVERY.

Lisa followed her heart and head to become an entrepreneur. Her Stand is for the power of enabling connections to change lives. Her decade destination is to be known as the Brené Brown of *Social Entrepreneurship* **Activating** <u>Connections</u> BETWEEN BUSINESS, PEOPLE, AND TECHNOLOGY.

Tina, our accomplished therapist, has a Stand to help create conditions for people to know that they are enough. Her decade destination is to be known as the Modern-Day *High Priestess* **Transforming** Fear INTO LOVE AND KINDNESS.

Stephene, our retired woman of all talents, is ready to embark on her next chapter without her husband's active involvement. Her decade destination is to be known as Compassionate *Guide* **Helping** Seekers LIVE FULLY.

Now it is your turn. Here are some Mad Lib suggestions to get your imagination going. The word choice is intentionally bold—use these in any combination or choose your own. You can even make up words. Complete this sentence, **"Wouldn't it be cool if ten years from now I was known by the people who love me, as well as those who count on me, as..."**

Exciting Adjective + *Powerful Subject* +
Dynamic Verb + Targeted Object +
EPIC OUTCOME

Exciting Adjective	+	*Powerful Subject*	+	**Dynamic Verb**	+	Targeted Object	+	EPIC OUTCOME

DECADE DESTINATION MAD LIBS

Adjective	Subject	Verb	Object	OUTCOME
Super	Architect	Inspire	Humans	Unconditional Love
Courageous	Shaman	Guiding	Leaders	Find Home
Modern-day	Wizard	Designing	Communities	Be Seen
Gracious	Medicine Woman	Cultivating	Mother Earth	Regenerate Life
Innovative	High Priest/ Priestess	Waking up	Seniors	Die in Grace
Shamanic		Connecting	Voiceless	Have Voice
Beloved	Warrior	Blessing	Children	Discover Their Divinity
Ecosystem	Elder	Constructing	Seekers	
Radiant	Builder	Illuminating	Sentient Beings	Live Fully
	Mid wife			Speak Their Truth

Here are more Mad Lib job descriptions that our Decade Gamers chose as their avatars to inspire their journey: "It would be so cool to be known as…"

- **Indestructible Force** leading people to realize a full life.
- **Creative Problem-solver** who turns hardship for women and girls into freedom and fully-lived lives.
- **Innovative Market Maker** inspiring women to be found, seen, heard, and equally represented.
- **Modern-day Goddess** helping others restore wholeness, balance, and workability.
- **Epic Storyteller** reconnecting humanity with Nature.
- **Courageous Wizard** cultivating humans to live fully and reach their potentials.
- The **Female Benjamin Franklin** who brings together disparate or warring people and ideas to make the impossible happen.
- **Radiant Influencer** who inspires others to rejoice in love and life and to make a difference.
- **Joyful Web Builder** inspiring humans to find their rhythm in the dance of life.
- **Potent Creator/Illuminator** transforming how people or entities live and demonstrate their truths.
- **Gracious Pro-Activist/Possibilitarian** igniting personal agency for a thriving people and planet.
- **Gracious Wizard** guiding leaders to be seen.
- **Amazonian Love Goddess** unfurling her story for the harmony of all.

- **Super Upstander** inspiring humans to have a voice and be seen.
- **Radiant High Priestess** inspiring people to lead with head and heart.
- **Free, Joy-Filled Rocket-Booster** bringing the best out of every person through Joy, Relevance, and Love.
- **Beloved Sherpa** igniting humans to grow their businesses and themselves.
- **Courageous, Empathetic Wizard** transforming human lives.
- **Joy Warrior** inspiring humans to value other humans.
- **Fierce Champion** of the marginalized, reimagining the center to include and amplify those on the periphery.
- **Delighted Oracle** galvanizing people to joyfully and fearlessly stretch their superpowers to realize the endless possibilities.
- **Courageous Innovator** developing leaders to become fully human.

Congratulations. You have been promoted. Your Mad Lib is your new job description. You now know where your real work lies—learning to be great at that unique yet essential job. When you get a promotion, it doesn't mean you know how to do your job, just that your employer is confident that you will master it. By the way, your promotion is in effect immediately. As soon as you envision how you and the world describe your epic character, she shows up for duty. The history of the future, your future, is beginning to write itself as you read this. You are now empowered to look at every choice—at home, at work, and in the world—through the lens of "What would [insert Decade Game Mad Lib] do?"

Rules of the Game:
You can't get there from here,
but you can get here from there.

Chapter 5

The Power of an Epic Game

I said it before, but it is important enough to repeat. Accomplished women have filled their dance card with worthy plans and projects. They are fully used up with goals, lists, to-dos, and deadlines. It's a herculean task to be on top of all the promises we have made to and for so many. It feels virtually impossible to think about the next ten years while consumed with what needs to be done in the next ten minutes. What is getting in the way? Here are my hypotheses:

- Women's muscles for naming and asking for what they desire and need for their own human flourishing are underdeveloped.

- The commitment to being "self-centered" feels selfish and is therefore actively shunned.
- Time horizons for planning are truncated, leaving women to react to what is coming at them as opposed to being strategic and intentional about their future.
- Even the most gifted women I know have a hard time choosing to be epic on their own without a tremendous amount of sustained encouragement from others.
- Women are afraid. Afraid to be wrong. Afraid of what others might think. Afraid something important will fall through the cracks, and it will be their fault. Afraid...
- Last, but not least, they have gotten lost in the "I should/I can't/I have to" universe and forgotten to have fun. A Good Girl's work is never done!

Play is a different energy than work. Play brings out your greatest creativity and imagination. Play reduces your fear of losing. Research in the power of play and gamification, from infants through to the end of life, is becoming mainstream in our understanding of human flourishing and innovation. In his book *Wonderland: How Play Made the Modern World,* Steven Johnson observes, "You will find the future wherever people are having the most fun...Play is the basis of all art, games, books, sports, movies, fashion, fun, and wonder—in short, the basis of what we think of as civilization. Play is what makes life lively."

Play is also essential to design. It allows for iteration and experimentation. It allows for feedback. It lights up parts of our brain that override the amygdala—that fight, flight, freeze place. Even losing is fun. I know you have experienced this. You are playing a challenging game that is filled with unknowns, surprises, unexplained detours. You fall through a trap door, slide down the chute, and lose your turn. "What do you do?" If you are like me, you jump right back in for the next round. Like other games you love to play repeatedly, there is no wrong move in the game of real life! Every move opens learning and new possibilities. There is only the next best move.

The more fun something is, the more you're willing to work on it. You don't buy a game because it's easy. If it is, it's too boring—it will sit on your shelf and gather dust. The more challenging the game, the more fun it is to play. Creating an epic life is a hard challenge. The strategies and tactics require you to be laser-focused about your dreams, choices, boundaries, and actions. For it to be an epic game, able to turn the seemingly impossible into the possible, it needs to be fun, albeit hard fun.

> "The Decade Game is fun, challenging, eye-opening, and empowering. Like a roller coaster, it provides a mix of thrills and suspense; when it's over, you immediately want to do it again!"
>
> **—PAULA, DECADE GAME CLASS OF 2019**

Don't confuse fun with happy or easy. Navigating through the game of a life worth living, fueled by love, passion, and purpose, brings an intensity to life that comes from playing your heart out. I know this firsthand. Midway through my Decade Game from fifty to sixty, I was at the pinnacle of my career as the Global Leader for the Life Sciences sector at EY, a $1 billion business that I helped build, serving global pharmaceutical and biotech companies with a wide range of consulting services. It was October 2006, and the phone rang just as I was walking out the door of our New York City apartment on my way to Mumbai, India, to launch a new initiative for EY and keynote a women's leadership conference. It was our doctor. I heard the sadness in his voice as he asked me to get my husband to join us on the call. I had to listen for a few minutes before the words began to register. My husband, Forrest, had three months to live.

The MRI had come back with clear evidence of esophageal cancer that appeared to be inoperable. When the phone call concluded, Forrest turned to me and said, "I am the battlefield, and you are my General—so time to get to work." It was a blessing that my newly acquired focus on the pharmaceutical industry had given me access to knowledge and relationships that helped me get Forrest into experimental clinical trials.

Luckily, he lived for another three years and had the time to complete important personal and professional projects that were dear to him. He also had a chance to take some well-deserved victory laps. In those three years, I spent a lot less time focusing on my career as I worked to shepherd Forrest through his trials. He was a beloved and accomplished minister of a large church in Manhattan. As the minister's wife, I found myself tending to the congregation who longed to walk alongside Forrest in his final chapter. Much of my heart time was devoted to his adult children, his mother, and his brother. I had promised Forrest that he would die at home. And so he did, in my arms, surrounded by his children, his ministerial colleagues, and his closest friends. At the moment he transitioned, a surprising thing happened. After sixty seconds of silence, I started to clap. After a pause, everyone joined me in a standing ovation. Forrest had done it—living for three more glorious years. And we had all played our part.

Beyond the seminal experience of breathing Forrest out of this world, the gift of the Decade Game showed up in three unexpected and miraculous ways:

First, the three years I attended to Forrest's final journey became the most profitable, highest growth years in my business career. I learned, by necessity, to show my vulnerability— to ask for help, to remove myself from the center stage spotlight, to trust my team—and they delivered. In essence, I grew into a heart-based leader as I let go of all my armor.

Second, Forrest didn't worry about me. He knew that I would be sad when he died, but he was confident I would not despair. He understood how deeply I trusted the process of my Decade Game to always find meaning and purpose in the millions of possible permutations that I could play with that would contribute to my family, my community, and the world at large. He was confident that my mourning process would ennoble my life. He told me I had given him a precious gift. He did not have to spend his dying time worrying about what would happen to me. With that gift, he was able to put all his energy into dying a good death.

Last, and most magical of all, my Decade Game journey brought me to Rob. After working together at EY for a decade, in 2005 Rob and I discovered that he and Forrest had been at Harvard Divinity School together in the 1970s and had even interned together at the same church in Boston. Neither of them knew I existed, yet both were destined to marry me. I hadn't used Forrest's surname in my professional work, so Rob had no idea who I was married to. Six weeks before Forrest's diagnosis, Rob and I stumbled on the connection during a spiritual conversation we were having as we worked on a project. Six weeks before that fateful call from Forrest's doctor, I reconnected the two of them at an event we were hosting at our apartment for Hillary Clinton during her second run for the Senate. Throughout Forrest's challenging illness, Rob and I continued to work together. Forrest used to say that the only thing that can never be taken away from you is the love you give away before you die. Forrest died on the day after his sixty-first birthday. In 2012, three years after Forrest passed away, and in the waning days of my fifty to sixty Decade Game, I gave my heart away to Rob in marriage.

An epic life is possible when your heart is open wide with the awe and humility of the miracle of our lives that is sandwiched in between the two great mysteries of birth and death. Forrest also preached that we should hope for the chance of a broken heart in our lives to understand the beauty of love. Good grief is an essential part of an epic life. EPIC! is an embodied feeling that comes when we are playing full-out in a game of our own choosing, even with its trap doors.

The game loses its luster, however, if you feel the game is rigged against you. My experience is when you're feeling frustrated, anxious, fearful, uncertain, compressed, or contained by life, chances are you are playing someone else's game. Decades of playing the Decade Game have taught me that it is my choice to have life happen "for" me, not "to" me. Then, whatever may come, an EPIC! journey promises the hardest fun of your life.

The First Move

We start by taking the first step required of any board game—open up and explore the game board, become familiar with the moving parts and pieces, and do a cursory review of the rule book to understand strategies on how to win and tactics on how to move your game piece.

Here is a wide-angle shot of the game board, which is in the form of a temple. Great news! Notice that you have already started to sketch out your Decade Game board.

- You have reflected on your Foundation in your Story So Far.
- You have begun to think about your Stand, which is the top, overarching ceiling of the entire temple.
- You have contemplated your ten-year journal entry as well as your decade destination (your Mad Lib) in Chapters 2 and 4.

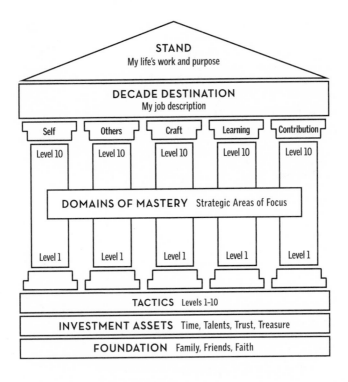

Congratulations—those elements can be tough to nail down. With these future beacons in place to illuminate our play, we turn to each area of our lives to name the transformational shift that is worth investing a decade of our time, trust, treasures, and talents—The Domains of Mastery.

More great news! The secret sauce of the Decade Game is that there are 87,600 hours in a decade. Even if you sleep eight hours a night (which I do and would highly recommend), it leaves over 50,000 hours of awake time. Malcolm Gladwell's 2008 bestseller *Outliers* popularized the "10,000-hours rule," originally coined by the Swedish psychologist K. Anders Ericsson. This rule posits that it takes about 10,000 hours of practice to become an expert in any field. So, let's do the math. In the Decade Game, you can become a world expert in five distinct yet related domains of mastery in ten years and still sleep eight hours a night. These domains of mastery are represented in the five pillars of the temple. They are the heart of the game and cover the five main areas of your life:

DOMAINS OF MASTERY

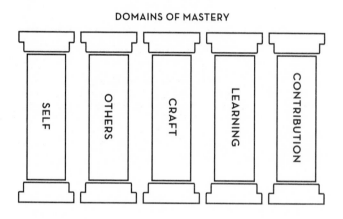

- SELF: The domain of your emotional, physical, spiritual, and positive sense of self.
- OTHERS: Representation of your one-on-one relationships and patterns with your family and friends.
- CRAFT: Your "occupational" work to become a master craftsman in your chosen field.
- LEARNING: Guiding your commitment to follow your curiosity to learn (and unlearn) about the real world.
- CONTRIBUTION: Your investments of your wealth, wisdom, work, and worldly connections to the work of other masters who have a similar Stand to yours.

Now, look at the top of each pillar annotated in the game board as L10 for Level 10. This is where you imagine an iconic event or situation that would describe the achievement of mastery in that domain that would require ten years to attain. It should be a super-stretch goal that would take you the full ten years to achieve. It is like a video game. You buy the game for its Level 10 epic objective, although you start playing it at Level 1. But more on that later as the next five chapters are devoted to a deep dive into each of these domains of mastery and tactics for playing. But first, let's explore strategies for winning.

Strategies for Winning

The Decade Game board is just a model to hold key concepts. Like all models in the design process, e.g., a model airplane, the model is not reality, just a depiction of certain aspects of reality that could be important. All models are, by definition, wrong (i.e., an incomplete version of reality) but occasionally can be useful. "Winning" in the Decade Game requires understanding the underlying concepts that make this imaginal game magical in "real" life.

Model Magic: The five domains of mastery describe a model of transformation that starts with Self and Others. Imagine the pillars nesting in each other, like a Russian "matryoshka" doll: a doll within a doll within a doll. The first pillar is at the core, influencing and shaping the next one, and so forth.

The heart of the model is YOU, the Self pillar. Your job is to do your psychological, physical, emotional, spiritual, and self-care work to construct your rehabilitation and re-membrance of your best self. What is my internal journey of transformation over the next ten years? What do I need to learn and experience to be in right relationship and integrity with myself and my faith? What is the transformation work of my heart, body, and soul that I am committed to practice and master? What would I do if I was not afraid?

"The Decade Game provided structure for me to be introspective, forcing me to face my true needs and passions."
—BETTY, DECADE GAME CLASS OF 2020

When you show up as your best self, then you are able to be in "right" relationship with the people you love. This is the second pillar of Others. Ironically, it is hardest to be your best, most evolved self with the people you love the most. That is where our deepest wounds lie. This pillar requires you to answer tough questions. What is my trans-formation work with my family, friends, colleagues? What is the repair work? What is the forgiveness work? Where am I doing their work instead of letting them do their own work? What are my healthy boundaries? How can I create conditions in the way I relate that invites them to be their best selves?"

The last three domains of Craft, Learning, and Contribution are about being in right relationship with "the collective," the world at large. Becoming more adept and skillful at managing your triggers, traumas, and negative patterns of self and family allows you to leave "home" liberated to do your best work in the world.

The third pillar of Craft is what you normally think of when you describe your job. In the Decade Game, we have broadened the scope of your "job" to encompass all the pillars. This pillar poses a more sophisticated question. What is your unique offering that reflects both the genius of what you do and how you do it in a way that brings forth goodness into the world? How are you a master craftsman amidst other colleagues who have similar technical skills or training, e.g., how do you differentiate? What is game-changing about what you want to "do" in the world? The objective of this domain is to be fully equipped to grow in mastery in your career and/or your community.

The fourth pillar is the domain of Learning. Although the act of learning is a key component in Self, Others, and Craft, it takes on a different meaning here. This is where you place all the experiences you want to have purely for the love of adventure, curiosity, pleasure, and erudition, like travel, art, hobbies, and reading. This is also the domain of unlearning, unknowing, and decolonizing your understanding of the world as you knew it so as to relearn from a deeper place of wisdom. This pillar guides you in an open inquiry. What gets my creative juices flowing? What hobbies have I ignored or experiences have I foregone because I was too busy?" What would I love to learn if only I had the time? This domain expands your horizons by being curious about what the world can teach you.

Contributions is the last domain of mastery. In your first four pillars, you are building your own mastery. Here you are scanning for other masters in the form of leaders and/or organizations that are building their mastery in service of a Stand that is complementary to yours. And they need your masterful gifts, talents, and wisdom to be complete. Who are the impactful leaders and organizations that are doing great work in…? How can I focus my philanthropic approach over the next decade? Where can I contribute my superpowers to other master change-makers who need them? In this domain, you are contributing your best self to society-at-large.

These five domains of mastery are distinct yet connected. Mastery in each influences the journey of mastery in the other pillars. They each resonate with your new Mad Lib identity, pave the way to your decade destination, and are different expressions of living your Stand. To increase your chances of experiencing an epic decade, you need to devote an equivalent amount of effort to name and pursue excellence in each of these domains instead of over-privileging one at the expense of others. For you overachievers, don't get anxious. You don't have to be working on each domain at the same time. You have all the time in the world—50,000 hours—to fit the puzzle pieces together in a masterful way.

Naming Magic: Remember when you would go into a toy store looking for a great new game? The name of the game gave you an idea of the type of adventure you would be on. Monopoly, Clue, Stratego, Candyland. Your decade destination is the meta mastery name of the Decade Game, to which all roads lead. However, each domain of mastery is a game within the Game. Each pillar needs a customized name, a title, for the way you would describe what the transformational shift would look like and feel like if you were able to win in that game of your choosing. Each pillar has its own epic objective (shown as L10 on the above model), requiring lots of game moves, along with setbacks, to fully manifest your destiny. The pillar name should be short, evocative, bold, and fill you with hope, clarity, and liberation. The name should also be your mantra and guide for what you say "yes" to and, as importantly, what you say "no" to. This new pillar title represents the vision of your magical trajectory.

As an example, let's look at Lisa's Decade Game board to see how she named her pillars and how they contribute to her Stand and decade destination. Note that each pillar has an iconic title that evokes Lisa's strategy for winning in that pillar as a stand-alone quest.

Lisa's decade destination is to be known as the Brené Brown of social entrepreneurship activating connections between business, people, and technology to change lives. She chose Brené Brown as her avatar. She was inspired by how Brené turned her experience in recovery and her job as a professor into a huge contribution as a renowned American researcher, story-teller, professor, lecturer, author, and podcast host who popularized the power of vulnerability. Lisa named her Self pillar, "Golden Guideposts," which comes from Brené's pronouncement of the ten Golden Guideposts for a wholehearted life. By giving her Self this title, Lisa is stating her intention to gain mastery in the cultivation of her authenticity, trust, self-compassion, resilient spirit, etc., while she lets go of all the self-doubt and other stories that no longer serve her. Lisa has a story behind the title of each pillar that captures the vision of how she will know herself and be known by family, friends, and colleagues after a decade devoted to her metamorphosis.

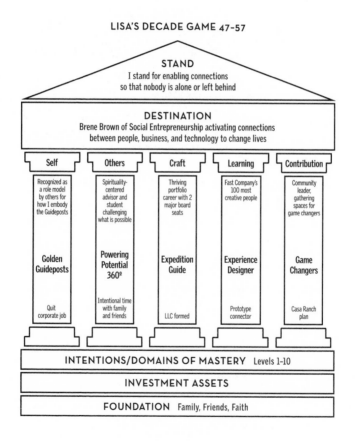

LISA'S DECADE GAME 47-57

STAND
I stand for enabling connections
so that nobody is alone or left behind

DESTINATION
Brene Brown of Social Entrepreneurship activating connections
between people, business, and technology to change lives

Self	Others	Craft	Learning	Contribution
Recognized as a role model by others for how I embody the Guideposts	Spirituality-centered advisor and student challenging what is possible	Thriving portfolio career with 2 major board seats	Fast Company's 100 most creative people	Community leader, gathering spaces for game changers
Golden Guideposts	Powering Potential 360º	Expedition Guide	Experience Designer	Game Changers
Quit corporate job	Intentional time with family and friends	LLC formed	Prototype connector	Casa Ranch plan

INTENTIONS/DOMAINS OF MASTERY Levels 1-10

INVESTMENT ASSETS

FOUNDATION Family, Friends, Faith

Note that as Lisa contemplated the question "Wouldn't it be amazing if…" for each pillar, she was able to visualize specific achievements at the end of the decade, her Level 10s, that delighted her. One of my mantras is, "If you can name it, you can claim it (and charge for it!)." Make sure your naming of the pillar title and Level 10s are a stretch, as epic as you can imagine. They should create nervous excitement in your body. These "names" should have you shake your head in amazement at your boldness. Yet, part of you should be nodding your head, "Yes! Why not!" So, imagine the award dinner, or the publication of a *New York Times* bestseller, or hosting the most amazing family reunion, or midwifing the revitalization of a beloved community. You will most likely find hints to the right iconic name for your pillars and Level 10s by rereading your decade journal entry that you imagined in Chapter 2.

In subsequent chapters, we will dive into each pillar to better understand what your work of mastery might be and how to name each pillar in a way that describes the transformational shift you are playing for.

Mastery Magic: It's liberating to know you can become a world expert in almost any area you choose by devoting only one-fifth of your waking hours over the decade and that you have enough waking hours to choose five different areas of your life—even if you are starting from a standing stop. While this math magic is helpful, it does not fully explain the power of a well-invested decade of time.

The starter ingredients to create the alchemy of mastery are passion, time, and innate skill. Mastery requires a few more ingredients for its secret sauce. In *So Good They Can't Ignore You,* author Cal Newport argues that super successful people are as good as they are because they're experts at *practicing.* They work at "deliberate practice" and push themselves to the limits of their skills. He posits that "follow your passion" doesn't work as well as "get good at something and your passion will follow." It turns out that the harder you work at mastery of something valuable, with a commitment to not settle for "good enough," the more passionate you will become. You also become better at what you practice. And you are always practicing something—even bad habits and old stories. In the Decade Game, what you do for a living is build mastery—experiences, knowledge, skills, insights, and relationships—in the five domains of mastery that advance your epic quest.

In *Focus: The Hidden Driver of Excellence*, celebrated psychologist and journalist Daniel Goleman (best-known for his influential 1995 book *Emotional Intelligence*) illuminated a complex truth behind the "10,000-hour rule." The secret ingredient is the qualitative difference in *how* you pay *attention*, not the quantitative measure of clocking in the hours. A vital ingredient is having experts and coaches who provide guidance and feedback loops. This type of coaching helps you recognize errors and learn how to self-correct for them in the future. These teachers also provide you with the positive recognition and encouragement for your commitment to mastery. As discussed in Chapter 3, building mastery and being recognized in a positive way by people "in the know" is critical to fueling your ambition to stretch, no matter how challenging the task. To build mastery, you need to practice with masters.

Additionally, according to Goleman, the optimal kind of attention requires a top-down clarity of what mastery looks like. This is activated by the power of specific visualization and grounded imagination expressed in your Stand, Mad Lib destination, and your Level 10s for each domain. Goleman writes,

> Paying full attention seems to boost the mind's processing speed, strengthen synaptic connections, and expand or create neural networks for what we are practicing…The experts concentrate actively on those moves they have yet to perfect, on correcting what's not working in their game, and on refining their mental models of how to play the game…Those at the top never stop learning.

The domains of mastery incorporate all this wisdom—passion, deliberate practice, role models and mentors, a vision of what greatness looks like, and a set of actionable tactics to guide your decisions and choices. The pillars also act as force multipliers. Your success in one area motivates and activates success in others. For example, when Lisa lives according to Brené Brown's Golden Guideposts, practicing self-compassion and letting go of perfection, she is better equipped to empower potential in everyone she meets. This fuels her Others pillar, which is entitled "Powering Potential 360." She is then ready to lean into her Craft pillar as an Expedition

Guide to perfect her ability to activate connections between people, business, and technology—all in service of her Stand.

Taken together, the pillars work with and on each other as they represent adjacent and simultaneous workstreams for the same job description—your decade destination. Steven Johnson, in his book *Where Good Ideas Come From: The Natural History of Innovation,* describes this phenomenon as "the adjacent possible."

> The adjacent possible is a kind of a shadow future,
> hovering on the edges of the present state of things,
> a map of all the ways the present can reinvent itself.

Citing the story of Darwin's theory of natural selection, Johnson observes that world-changing ideas generally evolve over time as *slow hunches* rather than sudden breakthroughs. Slowly working on these hunches over time, one move at a time, pillar on pillar, for a decade opens up a world of possibilities.

Level 1 Magic: You don't have to wait a decade or a year to start winning. By starting with the right story so far and having set up your game board with a clear vision of what epic success looks like, the winning has already started. You now have everything you need to start playing. Just like in a video game, you plunge in at Level 1 and start exploring the new environment. Start by choosing an action or decision that is currently within your power, resources, and capability. It is a baby step toward the future that incorporates a tiny bit of the magic promise of your Level 10 goals. We call this type of move "a tiny mighty" because it is totally doable in practice but is pregnant with your dream. In planning your first move, remember the rule: **"You can't get there from here, but you can get here from there."** This tip reminds you that you need 10,000 hours to reach your pillar goal—the There—which can seem daunting. However, you are absolutely equipped today to play a tiny mighty that is doable yet feels epic because your future self has chosen it. And she knows the score.

I saw this in action recently with thirty-five-year-old Cynthia, who was visiting with family in New Orleans. She had been pining for years to move from Boston, where she grew up, to New Orleans. She hated the Boston weather, felt constrained socially with the formality of the culture, and was ready for a change of pace. However, thirty-five years of inertia are a powerful force. The logistics seemed daunting, especially as we were still in the middle of the pandemic. Cynthia didn't want to disappoint family members still in Boston. She was concerned that her boss wouldn't agree to her continuing to work virtually (even though she had done it successfully for over a year). To level the playing field between past and future, I suggested she look at houses in New Orleans to move from the hypothetical to a more fully envisioned future. Cynthia fell in love with a few of the houses she checked out in her price range. But as the old stories of doubt started replaying in her mind, I saw the excitement begin to drain from her face. To break the fall, I asked her to travel to the future. "What would the forty-five-year-old Cynthia decide and advise?" The thirty-five-year-old was stuck, but the forty-five-year-old was clear. The next day she called her boss and said without hesitation or asking permission, "I'm moving to New Orleans but would love to stay in my job that I love." His response, "Great. Congratulations. I wish I could move to New Orleans!" A great example of a tiny mighty.

Every thirty days, or even every day, you can plot a new tiny mighty in each pillar. For example, a tiny mighty can be a decision to start meditating for five minutes a day (Self), call a loved one to have a difficult conversation (Others), say "yes" to a difficult project (Craft), sign up for an online workshop (Learning), or go to a community meeting (Contribution).

It's important to remember that the Decade Game isn't about mapping out the whole ten years in advance, knowing what each level will entail. A well-played Decade Game is a commitment to be great, inspired by your dreams, and show up as your best self at whatever you are doing **right now**. *There is no wrong move in the Decade Game.* Just good decisions and healthy choices on where to go next. Expect to have thousands of tiny mighty moves over the course of the decade. One best practice is to review your game board once a month. If you haven't taken at least one tiny mighty in each pillar, you are sitting on the sidelines.

Putting It Together

You now have the key components of the Decade Game board as well as the strategies for winning. Here is a review:

1. Take a Stand for your Purpose.

   - What is your theory of change about how the world gets better in a way that calls for your unique contribution?
   - This is your Life's Work.
   - Test it with the sentence, "The world gets better when..."

2. Imagine your Decade Destination.

   - Write a 600-word journal entry set ten years into the future.
   - How will you be known to yourself, the people who love you, and those who count on you based on your superpowers in action?
   - Write a short new job description for yourself in this format: Exciting Adjective + *Powerful Subject* + **Dynamic Verb** + Targeted Object + EPIC OUTCOME
   - This is your **Job Description** that you will work for the next decade to "earn."

3. Choose the Five Pillars that prioritize and name your journeys of discovery and mastery in Self, Others, Craft, Learning, and Contribution to other Masters.

   - Name each of the pillars for the shift that you desire to make—this is your designated "work" to do.

- This is the work in which you will invest your time, treasure, and talent to build mastery and recognition.
- These are your committed Domains of Mastery.

4. Imagine your Level 10 Mastery Icon for each Pillar.

   - What is an iconic event in ten years that would signal Level 10 Mastery and would take you ten years to accomplish?
   - This is your Epic Quest for each Pillar—the "big" work to be done.

5. Commit to a Level 1 Action every thirty days.

   - Practice getting here from there.
   - Put hope into action.

Exercise: My Decade Game

Time for your first draft. Jot down some notes and then read on.

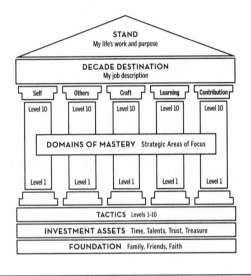

Rules of the Game:
If you can't have fun with a problem,
you can never solve it.

Section III

Playing For the Epic Win

From this hour I ordain myself loos'd of limits and
    imaginary lines,
Going where I list, my own master total and absolute,
Listening to Others, considering well what they say,
Pausing, searching, receiving, contemplating,
Gently, but with undeniable will, divesting myself of
    the holds that would hold me.
I inhale great draughts of space,
The east and the west are mine, and the north and
    the south are mine.
I am larger, better than I thought,
I did not know I held so much goodness.
All seems beautiful to me,
I can repeat over to men and women
You have done such good to me I would do the same
    to you,
I will recruit for myself and you as I go,
I will scatter myself among men and women as I go,
I will toss a new gladness and roughness among them,
Whoever denies me it shall not trouble me,
Whoever accepts me he or she shall be blessed and
    shall bless me.

    —WALT WHITMAN, from "Song of the Open Road"

Chapter 6

Self

Transformation Is an Inside Job

Cheryl described herself to me when we first met as "an indoor cat." She had a timorous air about her. She had finally achieved remission from the cancer that had rocked her world for the last two years. On top of that, after the passing of both her parents and years of an unhappy marriage, she was in year three of divorce proceedings. Our "indoor cat" only had a few close friends. In her professional career, she had always been in support roles to assist other people's dreams. Their dreams were big—like ending world hunger and saving the Amazon rain forest—and they captured her devotion and commitment. But her dreams had become small.

I love the name that Cheryl assigned to her work of transformation in Self—The Cool Alley Cat. Cool cats are hip, modern, and avant-garde. Alley cats have a broad, unbounded range of action, always venturing, exploring, defying house-bound rules. The name you give your work of Self can be evocative, expressive, inspiring, and, yes, "cool." We are naming the hardest possible work—work you haven't yet had the stamina and fortitude to explore and sustain. But remember, the more challenging the game, the more fun it is to play. Your desired shift in Self should make you gasp and giggle. As soon as your pillar name is set, you are immediately playing the game as your mind starts imagining what this could possibly mean for you. Like playing dress-up as a kid, as soon as the costume is on, you become it. "What would the Cool Alley Cat do in this situation?" is a very different energy than "Sigh…I'm just an indoor cat."

Cheryl's self-work is about healing her mind, spirit, and body so that she is a "living example" of what it means to have the power to heal herself. Every day she looks for opportunities to know that she is enough. She has completed her divorce, cleaned up her financial complications with people she didn't know how to say "no" to, identified where she has invited toxic situations, structured a preventive regimen to keep the cancer at bay, and is a champion for her own well-being. The Self domain of mastery is the anchor of her temple and her transformation.

Self

Level 10: I am a living example of my stand: a beacon for people. As Gandhi said, "My life is my message." My home and my garden are a showcase for healing and well-being. My personal relationships are all in restorative health. I have total health of my mind, my body and my spirit

Personal Health and Well-being

Level 1: Be completely and totally healed

The exploration of the domain of Self reminds me of the brilliant Pixar film *Inside Out* that takes you inside the mind of Riley, an eight-year-old girl who has been uprooted from her Midwest life and moved to San Francisco. She is not happy. When meeting her, you get a chance to meet the anthropomorphic avatars of her core emotions—Joy, Fear, Anger, Disgust, and Sadness—and see how they argue and compromise on how best to navigate a new city, house, and school. They are like the chatty, opinionated roommates that live in our minds, insisting on being heard and never shutting up.

I suspect that we all have our own versions of these crazy roommates. They have their own origin stories, each with their authentic truth and a specific job to do. This phenomenon is best described by a relatively new addition to the therapeutic self-development portfolio, Internal Family Systems (IFS). Developed by Richard Schwartz, IFS is an evidence-based model of psychotherapy based on the theory that our mind is naturally "multiple," and that is a good thing. Our inner parts that make up the family of "me" contain valuable qualities, roles, and responsibilities that have been the allies of our core Self. These individual parts have had their unique position to play in managing, warning, controlling, firefighting, and comforting the Self. However, as the Self heals and grows, these distinct parts can integrate into the whole and enter a more mature, less cantankerous, regenerative relationship. In IFS, all parts are welcomed, honored for their service, and, at the right time, decommissioned or promoted to an advisory, not operating, capacity.

I described in Chapter 2 the Good Girl that lives in every woman I know. My Good Girl had an important supervisory job—to make sure I was loved and safe. To perform her job well, she delegated the tasks to a capable team of experts. For example, she learned early on how not to make men angry by calling on "Darling Girl" to be as sweet and loving as possible. She enlisted a part I call "City Hall," who decided to give away the key to my body boundaries at an early age so as to avoid any conflict with men. To receive a different kind of adoration, she hired, on my behalf, a "Rock Star" stage manager who made sure I could always grab the mike and take center stage to deliver a stellar performance.

I am not a therapist, just a recovering Good Girl who has had to navigate the world of Goldilocks to recover my power. The Decade Game is not a professional therapeutic methodology trying to break down and solve the psychopathology of how our parts have helped us survive. Rather, it is a framework and model that employs "psycho-mythology" to sketch the outlines of a new epic identity for our heroine and recommission all her parts for this adventure. The epic objective of the Self pillar is to embody a marked exponential shift from surviving to thriving.

Many of the outwardly successful, highly functioning women I know who have simultaneously navigated home and work arenas have been willing to accept the condition of being "half-healed." I see it often in the Decade Game Master Classes. These multitalented women are grappling with their own hidden core wounds that have alienated them from their bodies, emotions, souls, and truth. Many of them have suffered from sexual abuse and/or the traumas related to parental emotional abuse, alcoholism, or domestic violence, which required them to be the mother/protector of themselves, their siblings and/or moms at an early age. They have oftentimes inherited the intergenerational unresolved trauma of their mothers and grandmothers.

The Self pillar calls on us to name the emotional, physical, and spiritual self-care to lead to our own recovery. Without mastery of the domain of the Self, the temple rests on shaky ground. Let's look at some examples from a 2021 Master Class of women spanning the ages of thirty to seventy-two. We started by examining the core beliefs that have powered our story of Self. Core beliefs can be positive or negative and determine to what degree we see ourselves as worthy, safe, competent, powerful, and loved. These beliefs come from a story we told ourselves or believe to be true, usually rooted in the past, whether these stories still serve us or not. Common negative beliefs are built on a mindset of scarcity and are themes and variations of "I am not enough"—not good enough, smart enough, loveable enough, worthy enough…Or, I am "too much"—too loud, sensitive, ambitious, selfish, arrogant. Positive core beliefs are built on a sufficiency mindset—I am enough, you are enough, we are enough. They sound like these:

- I am brave and can do this.
- My voice should be heard.
- I can do anything I put my mind to.
- I can trust my heart and intuition.
- I am free to be me.
- I am desirable.
- I'm not here to be average; I'm here to be awesome.

Negative core beliefs act as an anchor dragging down our possibilities. Our positive core beliefs act as superpowers that fuel our effectiveness in the world and help quiet the "I can't" and "I am afraid" voices.

Our participants were asked to name the negative core belief that holds them back the most. They also identified the superpowers they relied on to fuel magic in their lives. As our participants drummed up the courage to confess their most debilitating negative core beliefs with each other, healing started immediately. They saw their own tears in each other's eyes. These beliefs and concerns had a job to do at the time, keeping the Self safe enough to be able to continue to learn, experiment, test, and develop strengths and superpowers.

Here are some of their insights. Pay attention to the paradoxical universe we inhabit! Our negative core beliefs are valuable partners in birthing the empathy that turned into the same woman's superpower and genius. What alchemy!

NEGATIVE CORE BELIEF	MY SUPERPOWER
I am unlovable.	I help people get engaged and contribute their ideas.
Others are more important than me.	I get past all roadblocks.
I am not enough.	I have an intrinsic leadership quality and help Others feel heard, respected, and empowered.
It is not safe to speak out.	I am a Master Storyteller.
I am not good enough.	I help people achieve things beyond imagination.
Female beings are here to serve.	I am a joyful and laser-focused creator of community experiences.
Others are more than I am.	I ask questions that make Others feel valued and engaged.
I am not enough to go for my dreams.	I am a light-speed synthesizer and community creator.
Failure is not an option.	I help people tame the complex and feel loved while they do it.

NEGATIVE CORE BELIEF	MY SUPERPOWER
I will never be enough.	I illuminate the known and unknown so group genius and new possibilities emerge.
I am not worth people's efforts.	I am a justice fighter.
I am too intimidating.	I have the magic eye to see what is longing to happen.
I am not worthy.	I am mission-driven and ennoble communities.

My negative core belief was "I am too much." I always felt the necessity to "dim my light" so that others could shine (i.e., too much Rock Star). When I own that I am enough, I stop trying so hard to deliver the performance of the century. I shine the spotlight on others, and magic happens.

The title you give the Self pillar expresses how it would feel if you finally let go of the negative core beliefs that no longer serve you and could lean fully into a decade of courageous self-exploration. I love the word "courage." It comes from the Latin root "cor" and the French "coeur"—heart. It means to go forward with your heart in your mouth at times of doubt, fear, and uncertainty. Much of our unresolved trauma is embedded in our subconscious and bodies. Our bodies know the real score. I know mine does.

When I was eight, I was molested by a stranger on my first

solo plane flight from my home in Syracuse to New York City to visit my grandparents. When I was fifteen, I lost my virginity in a date rape by the older brother of one of my friends. I never mentioned either of these two incidents to anyone, including my parents, until I was in my sixties. When I was thirty-two, I pushed myself too hard trying to close a major deal and miscarried. At the time, I was unwilling to take an "off-ramp" from work for fear that it would derail my career. This decision haunts me to this day. I could go on and on. So could you.

It is not just the physical assaults and trauma on our person that need to be healed. It is the stories that we have told ourselves to survive and thrive that cry out for a retelling. Our sense of self, the ego, is just the defensive playbook that supports our decisions on how best to show up so that we can survive and be loved. Except what got us here won't get us there. In essence, the body learns, the heart feels, and the mind interprets. It's time to go on offense. Transformation is truly an inside job.

I had a full, embodied experience of the power of Self-transformation in 2013 as I kicked off my Decade Game 60–70. As I contemplated my upcoming marriage to Rob, I made an unusual honeymoon choice. Instead of sitting on a beach in Fiji, I suggested that we climb Mount Kilimanjaro. Neither my husband nor I was a climber. Given my Mad Lib title of being known as an "Organizational Shaman Inspiring Humans to Lead Epic Lives," I thought, "What would a Shaman do?" She would not be drinking Mai-Tais on her honeymoon. I knew that climbing Kili would be an experience that would be as much an internal spiritual journey as it was a physical challenge.

In the local language, Kilimanjaro means difficult journey, and so it was. The ascent was a rigorous seven-day climb, thirty-seven miles, 19,000 feet in elevation, ten to twelve hours a day, through many different climate zones—tropical, savanna, rain forest, and winter (think glacier!). Given the elevation, the cold, very little sleep as we clung to the mountain at night shivering in our tent, and my relative lack of training, I felt weak on the sixth day as we prepared to summit. We left base camp at 15,500 feet before dawn, intending to reach the summit by 4 p.m. Knowing that it's in the descent that most climbing accidents happen, this plan would allow us to get back to base camp before nightfall.

Given my snail's pace, at 4 p.m., we were not close to the summit. I was exhausted. Every breath was tortuous. I had to stop after every two steps. My heart was beating out of control. The color of my face was a scary shade of green-gray, and my husband insisted that we stop and reconsider. "Sweetheart, we can't keep going this way. You will either have a heart attack or we will reach the summit at night and then have the treacherous journey back to camp in complete dark." Our two Tanzanian guides gave us some hot sweetened tea and space to consult. That is where I learned "parts theory." Rob asked me to go inside myself, consult my body, and determine which part of me was able and "fit for purpose" to complete the ascent. The masculine energy and old ego stories of "you must perform," "you must get to the top" fell away. Instead of getting to the top, my destination became "getting to the center." The wisdom of mother earth, mother mountain, and the feminine energy of trust rose up, and I knew what to do. My body told me I could trust my quadricep muscles and my breath to meld with the gravity of the mountain to carry me to the top and that I could rest my heart.

Imagine climbing at a sixty-five-degree angle. All you need to do is exhale, fall forward in a lunge, inhale and stand, then repeat. I was able to lunge for ninety minutes, slowly but without stopping, until I reached the summit and fell into my husband's waiting arms.

The work of the Self pillar is to liberate ourselves from the stories that have kept us from being fully in our power, connected to our purpose, and reveling in the enjoyment of our embodied liberation.

Let's check back in with Priya, our millennial software engineer, to see how she framed her Self pillar.

Priya was born and educated in India in a very traditional Indian family and culture. Now living in Chicago, she has worked for the same global technology solutions company for the last decade. She is married with a young daughter. Everything in her life is culturally traditional—the role of mother, the role of wife, the role of a software engineer, the role of women. Priya is quiet, soft-spoken, deferential, courteous, unassuming—at first meeting. Over the course of the Decade Game, she blossomed in front of our eyes. It was like watching the sped-up version of a seed, pregnant with possibilities, unfolding into the most beautiful flower. She views her Decade Game as a "Power Game." It is the power of a positive belief system born in her Self pillar that will contribute in every area of her life—home, work, and the world.

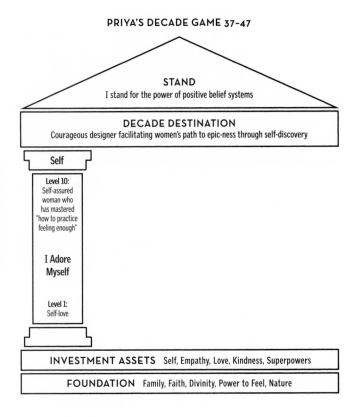

PRIYA'S DECADE GAME 37-47

STAND
I stand for the power of positive belief systems

DECADE DESTINATION
Courageous designer facilitating women's path to epic-ness through self-discovery

Self

Level 10:
Self-assured woman who has mastered "how to practice feeling enough"

I Adore Myself

Level 1:
Self-love

INVESTMENT ASSETS   Self, Empathy, Love, Kindness, Superpowers

FOUNDATION   Family, Faith, Divinity, Power to Feel, Nature

The name you give your Self pillar describes the seismic shift in the quality of your own presence at the end of a decade. A delicious, juicy, and inspiring You. Priya rose to the challenge with the title "I Adore Myself." What a declaration of sufficiency and power!

For some people, it's helpful to think about an epic character from mythic, historical, or current times that forecasts the embodiment of your future self. For example, Priya's twin sister, OJ, named her Self pillar "I am Durga." Durga is a Hindu goddess created to combat the evil demon Mahishasura. The trinity of Brahma, Vishnu, and Shiva came together to create a powerful female form with ten arms. Devotees worship Durga to gain positive energy, to cleanse their mind so as to attain purity and salvation. OJ chose goddess Durga to embody these virtues as the best version of herself.

> "The Decade Game brought alive for me the power and the magic of being you and setting deliberate intentions to live boldly and wholeheartedly."
> —OJ, DECADE GAME CLASS OF 2021

Here are a few more names that Decade Game participants have chosen to name their Self work in a way that quiets their negative story and names the quality of their presence when they activate their superpower.

NEGATIVE CORE BELIEF	SUPERPOWER	SELF PILLAR
From I am unlovable, yet	I help people get engaged	I AM JOYOUS SOUL
From I am not enough, yet	I have an intrinsic quality to help Others feel empowered	I AM DIVINE LIGHT
From I am not good enough, yet	I help Others achieve things beyond imagination	I AM COURAGEOUS EAGLE
I will never be smart enough, yet	I Illuminate the unknown so group genius emerges	I AM SENSUOUS GODDESS

At the conclusion of our workshop, Priya sent me a letter that included the following:

Thanks to decade game, I feel I have tools and a direction now to work on self.

I now look at my life's negative moments differently. I now see them as life experiences that I accept and acknowledge. I now have a self-talk that goes past it like an arrow saying I acknowledge you, but you are not my future. So stop ringing.

Earlier, I used to think I had nothing to offer to anyone and questioned my worthiness and ability to contribute or to even speak up. The brave space of decade games has helped me re-define myself. I was using old narratives that pulled my mood down and affected my self-worth. You changed that deeply settled mindset by helping me understand, about the stories we tell ourselves and how we can change the narrative.

The Decade Game is helping me discover my strengths. Earlier when I would think about my strengths, I felt I had none, but I have seen that after just few sessions into the decade games, I did have a list. I feel I am claiming them now.

We are a character of our own life story. The past character was flawed, built on other people's stories or my interpretations of those stories that don't serve me now. Since I am the storyteller, now I get to change my character, my way.

Doing the unfinished work of Self requires the fortitude of salmon swimming upstream. Society has conditioned remarkable women to excel at ensuring the absence of others' discomfort, at the expense of our own comfort. "Giving to others is better than receiving." "Be the rock and pour for others before you drink." "When the going gets tough, tough it out." "Be Superwoman." We are asked to do all this but, at the same time, "Don't be self-centered." Really?!

This domain is ALL about self-centering. There is still a little girl inside each of us who is asking to be nurtured and cared for so we are free to reconnect to the child-like joy and rapture of being alive. Consequently, the difficult work of this pillar is facilitated—meaning "to make easy"—with self-love, self-care, sensuous pleasures, fun, and self-centered commitment to heal. This is the "wake up" pillar. Instead of the common bed-time prayer that I used to recite as a child, "If I die before I wake…" the Self pillar posits a different question. "If I wake before I die…"

> "Now I lay me down to sleep,
> I pray the Lord my Soul to keep;
> If I should die before I 'wake,
> I pray the Lord my Soul to take."
> —THE NEW ENGLAND PRIMER

Getting Started: Naming Your Self pillar

In Chapter 4, I shared the power of "naming" and the fact that every pillar is a game within the Game. The name of your Self pillar labels the transformational shifts in your story of Self—spiritual, emotional, physical—that would become apparent to you and others once these shifts were mastered. Or, more simply said, who is the person you want to become and what transformation within you is needed for that to happen? How would you show up for yourself differently when you are in the flow of your best self?

Naming Convention: To name the Self pillar, you are answering the following question:

"Who am I? For me, I am _____."

Questions to consider

1. What strengths and superpowers have you built by navigating around your negative core beliefs?

2. What strategies and tactics allow you to find the "turn around" or "reframe"?

3. What would be possible if you honored the wisdom and insights that came from your negative core beliefs but acted on the positive core beliefs?

How would you "name" the transformation of your inner Self after a decade of acting on the positive stories?

Rules of the Game:
The trials and tribulations of the past
are the treasures that fund the future.

Chapter 7

Others

You Are How You Love

It was very hard for Janice to imagine what the future could be. She was just surfacing from a decade of caretaking for people she loved, shepherding them through their final passages. She'd lost her mother, grandmother, father, and her beloved sister. When the first distress call came about her mother's illness, Janice was working her way up the corporate ladder in New York as a marketing manager for a Fortune 500 company.

Janice had grown up in a suburb of Detroit, Michigan, where her father was a successful African American businessman in a predominantly white, white-collar industry. The relative power and privilege of this status came with a cost that many African American families are familiar with. The realities of trying to fit in, the pressure of trying to represent your race well, the reality of being "always on stage" placed most of the burden on Black professionals' shoulders to make white colleagues and neighbors comfortable with their co-existence. This had certainly been Janice's experience as well, navigating a path of being a distinct minority at undergrad, graduate school, and eventually in the workplace.

Her decade spent caring for her mother and the subsequent illnesses of her family were poignant yet grueling. With the death of her father, Janice received the gift and the burden of financial independence. She felt the daunting responsibility of making sure her survival and good fortune were put to good use. As women, and doubly so for women of color, our experience in a white man's world requires us to be constantly hitting the ball out of the park to justify our own seat at the table and, at the same time, represent our gender, race, and ethnicity well.

When I met Janice, she was tentatively emerging from her grief, happily married, and looking toward getting her life back on a track she could recognize. As you read in Chapter 2, an initial "game move" is to write your journal entry ten years into the future. This was a difficult exercise for Janice. I could tell how much she was longing for vast possibilities. Yet putting pen to paper created a lot of tears. I had a sense that she was afraid to dream. In deep reflection, Janice realized that she carried these tears as ancient sacraments of intergenerational dashed hopes. Making conscious choices about an epic future seemed momentous to her. She felt she was not just responding to her life's desire—but about changing the future story of her lineage in America, which started as an enslaved people.

Janice's sense of being connected with her ancestors, loved ones, and future generations underscores the breadth and depth of the second domain of mastery: Others. This relatedness pillar is not about the public at large. It is about your one-on-one relationships with the people you love. It is with our family of origin where we first feel the core emotions of love, fear, anger, shame, joy, safety, disgust. It is in relationship with these people—as protagonists, victims, persecutors, heroes, competitors, and bystanders—that we have built the stories of Self.

The mastery called for in the Others domain is the work of repair, renewal, reconciliation, re-engagement, revitalization, and re-membering. The objective is to deepen the relationships that mean the most to us and unlock the unconditional love that is ours to give and receive.

This pillar names the way you want your loved ones to experience your best self in a way that creates the possibility for them to show up as their best selves. The title you give this pillar points to the result of ten years of deepening relationships. It is crazy, but it is often hardest to be your best self with the people you love most in the world. It's amazing to me how easy it is for my sixty-nine-year-old self to fall back into the sullen fifteen-year-old during family get-togethers. Or find myself competing with my sixty-plus-year-old siblings for my ninety-plus-year-old mother's approval. Ironic but not surprising given that our entire life is a journey of recovery from our earliest experiences of conditional love. This pillar requires you to answer questions like, "What is my one-to-one transformational work with each of my family, friends, colleagues?" "How can I create conditions in the way I relate to them that invites them to be their best selves?"

This is not a static pillar based on what your work is today with your loved ones. It reflects the dynamic nature of the relationship developments over a decade. Most of our current and future loved ones will be in differing stages of their lives—moving from child to adolescent, adolescent to young adult, single to married, married to divorced, working to retired, healthy to sick. Each transition in your loved ones' lives changes your relationship possibilities and opens avenues for healing as you move through your own transitions and growth.

For example, all my children are now in their mid to late thirties and early forties. They have come into my orbit at different times. At age sixty, when I married Rob, I inherited two more stepchildren. This brought the number of adult children in my blended family to six—my two biological sons, my two stepchildren from my second marriage, and my two new stepchildren. As I write this on the cusp of turning seventy, the "kid" count is now eleven with the arrival of a son-in-law and four daughters-in-law who bring their own family histories and hurts with them. The future also is uncertain, with several of these relationships suffering from pandemic-related strains. Add to that, seven grandchildren in the last decade. My "job" with these three blended families is dynamic, to say the least. It turns out that blended families blend only so much, no matter the effort and intentions. Some want to be fully engaged in an extended family. Others, not so much.

Adding to the complexity, they are now all heads of their own household. Ten years ago, they were all psychologically and, in some cases, literally still part of my house. My work over the last decade has been to let go of thinking it's my job to fix their problems and contribute to their happiness. In their teenage years, I was consumed with making sure everyone had a shot at old age. Today I am no longer central to any of their lives. I've had to let go of my idea that I should be the matriarch on top of the clan actively dispensing my sought-after advice. Instead, they are living their own lives into which I am occasionally invited. This insight has required a lot of work on my part to change my expectations and behaviors to mirror this reality. And that work continues! It is never once and done.

This pillar includes every category of your loved ones—parents, siblings, children, grandchildren, and even, like Janice, ancestors. Mastery will require deft decisions in different ways over the evolving stages of you and your relations. Over the decades, based on my stage of life, I had set different macro intentions for the Others pillar. Here are a few more examples. As I designed my sixty to seventy decade, I had specific healing and repair intentions with my mom. Given that this game would span her eighty-four to ninety-four ages, it was reasonable to expect that it could be her last decade. I wanted to get as close to her as possible, which meant I would need to open up and be vulnerable. For most of my life, I had been a self-comforter. I inherited that from my mother. I knew that had to change if we were going to get closer. Fast forward—I have only in the last year shared with her some early traumas that I referred to in the last chapter. Finally ready, I was able to give her the gift of comforting me—a gift that both of us needed, but I had been afraid/unwilling to ask for half a century ago.

I also had a reputation in my family over the decades for "sucking the air out of the room" by my need for acknowledgment of my external accomplishments. Growing up, I felt that exceptional performance was required by me to be loved and adored. There was also an intergenerational pattern of competition amongst siblings. By focusing on my need for approval, I wasn't attentive to what was needed by my siblings for them to feel valued and honored by me. This required me to do my own soul retrieval work in my Self pillar so that I could show up differently without resentment felt by them or me. Resentment comes from the old French *resentir*, "feel again, feel in turn," and is a common bedfellow among siblings, given the nature of competition for parental love. The work of this pillar is to transcend the negative love patterns and find the golden place of mutual respect and compassion, where you are creating opportunities to "re-see" what is possible.

For these reasons, I named the Others pillar in my current game "Oasis." My intention was to let go of the past and future, stop trying to fix or solve anything for them, and just live in the present, ready to celebrate their presence. I imagined creating a physical and energetic space and grace that is always welcoming, always irradiating unconditional love, and clear about boundaries. A place for journeyers to rest, rejuvenate, bind up wounds, feel love, and have hope rekindled.

For many, this is the hardest pillar of all. This is the place to put into practice your own internal work of self-forgiveness, compassion, unconditional love, healthy boundaries, and emotional intelligence. This domain of mastery calls for creativity, courage, consciousness, and intentionality. You are committing to doing all the changing and shifting without any guarantee that your loved ones will change. There is no "meet me in the middle" in practicing unconditional love with healthy boundaries. There is no promise of immediate gratification. You are signing up for the long game.

This domain of mastery is a lynch pin in your metamorphosis to the next stage of your life. If you don't do this work with your loved ones, you bring any unfinished business and a boatload of emotional triggers into your work in the world. Left untended, this diminishes the power of your contributions. The Others pillar is the bridge that connects being in right relationship with Self to being in right relationship with the world—your Craft, Learning, and Contributions pillars.

Let's see how Janice connected the dots on her game board by envisioning her work of Others. Listen for how her future story helped illuminate possibilities in the present:

Janice's Stand: *I stand for the power of Truth, Liberation, and Sovereignty to ignite the full potential in all human beings and their sacred relationship to this planet.*

Janice's Decade Destination: *I am a Joyful Prophet and Way Shower shining a light on contemporary bondage, opening doorways to lasting freedom for all people.*

Janice is naming the shift in her relationship with Others as Soul Nourisher, creating and curating a magical and playful space. Her commitment is to shift her relationship energy from one of anxiety, worry, and caring to an energy that nourishes others' souls. This is not a small shift. The intergenerational trauma of bondage, her history of responsibility for making other people comfortable, and her decade of loss created the lens in which she "showed up" in relationships. The naming of the shift that she so desires reframed her understanding of what her job is—which is to lighten the load on others' shoulders by lightening her own load.

The blessing of this relatedness shift immediately liberated Janice into a different relationship with her family. Instead of being worn down by caregiving, she is lighting up with her mission to nourish souls, including her own. She is creating space and grace for play—for herself and the people she loves. After naming this pillar, Janice revised her decade journal entry to say this:

I'm filled with gratitude that the realm of play is such an integral part of my life. It's something that my parents, grandparents, and great- grandparents did not have the luxury or freedom to think about. Seriousness has its place, of course (particularly in my efforts to confront social and ecological injustices), but it took up way too much of my life prior to 2019. I feel more alive and vibrant now that I cherish the gift of play on a regular basis.

Exercise: The Relationship Shift

Here is a simple model. Name all the important relationships in your life today and hypothetically in the future (new child-in-law, grandchild, partner, best friend, etc.).

How old will they be in a decade, and what is the desired shift in the relationship that would happen if you were able to always show up as your best self? Is there an overall theme that could drive these desired outcomes? For example, do you need to detach from outcomes and become a "possibilist"? Is there a "meta" theme about moving from worry to trust? Maybe your transformational shift is about practicing healthy boundaries?

Person—Current Age	Age in 10 years	Desired Shift
Mom—75	85	More helpful
Sister—50	60	Less competitive
Son—28	38	Less worried
Partner—49	59	More accepting
Friend—45	55	Re-engaged
Future Daughter-in-Law	?	Candid supporter

Getting Started: Naming Your Others Pillar

This domain is about the shift the people you love (your one-on-one relationships) will observe, feel, relish, and cherish when they are with you. It is NOT their transformational shift (that is *their work*) but rather your shift that can create openings for the deepening of love, trust, honor, and respect. In this pillar, you detach from focusing on outcomes and become committed to possibilities. It will also reflect the healthy boundaries that you have established with each of them.

Naming Convention: Your Others pillar should be named for how you want to show up in a way that invites Others to respond accordingly. The name will reflect the enhanced and transformed quality of your presence for them that is the result of your intentional work.

How am I for you that invites you to be your best self? What name best describes me when I am most helpful to you? For you, I am _____.

Questions to Consider

1. Who are the five to ten relationships that you are committed to deepening in the next twelve months?

2. Imagine the story each will tell about you and how they each "feel" about themselves when they are with you.

3. What is the overarching theme of these stories that names your shift?

Rules of the Game:
It is not who you know but how you
are known for the way you love.

Chapter 8

Craft

You Are a Master Craftsman

When I met Kim, she seemed magical in every way. We met at a board dinner for Room to Read, a nonprofit organization globally focused on literacy and gender equality education in the developing world. Kim had a successful career as a Wall Street equities biotech analyst on the East Coast. She eventually moved west to continue to cover the emerging biotech industry. She married Ian, also an equities analyst, and had one son. Kim defines her profession as a portfolio career where she manages her different roles as an advocate, artist, investor, and activist. Kim shows up in the world as a totally together human. However, it turns out there is no such thing as a totally together human. And the "totally together humans" know this better than anyone.

Amidst Kim's triumphs and joys, she had suffered trials and loss. Her father passed away suddenly in 1993 when she was in her twenties, and her beloved brother died of cancer in 1994. The relationship with her mother, who married Kim's boss after her father died, lacked a closeness that always seemed to be slightly out of reach. Kim went to boarding school when she was seven and began, inadvertently, working on her invulnerability. She was determined to flourish, no matter what. At thirty-five, three months after a C-section, Kim was training to compete in a one-hundred-mile horseback race in Napa Valley when she and her horse tumbled down a steep ravine. She shattered her collarbone and ribs as well as seriously damaged her dominant right arm and shoulder. Fifteen years later, she is still aware of pain in her body.

Kim is a natural "recoverer." She instinctively looks for meaning in the present from the wounds of the past—an intuitive self-healer and self-comforter. She is exhilarated with the immense blessing and scope of her life. However, the many falls and recoveries masked a question that was seminal for her and for most women I know. "Am I Enough?"

Her goals for the Decade Game were to answer that question on an intellectual, spiritual, physical, and emotional level with the following intentions:

- Feel lighter.
- Learn to deepen relationships with her mother, husband, and son with more vulnerability.
- Better understand her gifts and push herself to grow.
- Have clarity on a blueprint that celebrates and illuminates what she considered her Prime of Life decade (mid-forties to mid-fifties).

Kim was seeking to make tangible what, as an artist, she could sense. There is a reason matter matters. To put something into tangible, visible form allows you to examine "the thing," to put it up to the light, to investigate it from different angles, and to know it is not going to disappear.

Artistically, Kim reimagined the game board for herself. In a model of her own creation, she captured her dreams, intentions, and commitment. She thinks about the Decade Game as a set of bylaws governing who she is, what she is made of, and what her imprint on the world can be. Kim describes it this way:

It is not a map. It is not a foundational system. It is a new way of thinking and being. It is as if this new image is the nucleus of each of my cells. I can heal myself and others with it, and I can envision and change energy with it. It is less about a destination of achievement in the traditional sense and more about being. It is a place from which to live and illuminate.

ILLUMINATOR
Integration   Balance   Sufficiency

Sacred Masculine   N   LIGHT

FIRE

AIR

SELF

LEARNING

OTHER

W   E

CONTRIBUTION

ENOUGH

CALLING

MAGICK

WATER

EARTH

DARK   S   Sacred Feminine

I stand to ignite and illuminate Enoughness.

△ = ritual or ceremony

This concept of illumination inspired Kim to draw her game board in the form of a six-pointed star. As she considered many of her choices, beliefs, and actions—as a professional, artist, activist, daughter, mother, wife—she was motivated by the search for breathing deeply into "enough" for herself and others.

Kim's Stand: *I stand to ignite and illuminate Enoughness so that we may each give uniquely to the world.*

Kim's Decade Destination: *To be known as The Illuminator of pathways for people to recognize themselves as Integrated, in Balance and Sufficient, Enough and Whole.*

The Craft pillar is tricky because people want to associate it with "my job." As a reminder, one of the key tenets of the Decade Game is that your job is NOT what someone is paying you to do. You have a much bigger job. It is to make sure that every experience and investment of your time, talents, treasures, and trust are milestones toward your decade destination and in service of your Stand.

To that end, I have purposely named this domain CRAFT and not "work" or "profession." In our performance culture, much of our identity is wrapped up in the way we are known at work and the fact that we spend more of our waking hours at work than any other place. Sometimes we call work our vocation, but that's not right either. Vocation comes from the Latin root *vocatio*, literally "a calling, a being called." In the Decade Game, your calling is your Stand—the entire epic quest of the game.

Having said that, one of the cardinal rules in the Decade Game is that at any point in time, if necessary, one of the pillars will be writing you a check. For women, financial stability is an essential design challenge for every decade. Without that, it is hard to be fully in control of your power, purpose, and pleasure. Usually, that source of stability comes from the Craft pillar in an area considered your job by your employer.

We think of the word craft as a hobby. More than traditional "work," a craft is something that you choose to do because it is fun, creative, and you are inspired to become accomplished at it. It is the workshop where you create a unique objet d'art based on your own combination of artistry, skill, and imagination. Several hundred years ago, craftsmen of every trade were considered artisans, whether they were blacksmiths, weavers, carpenters, or builders. The early predecessors of labor unions and professional associations were Craft Guilds. These artisans were each known for the specific hallmark of their work.

In designing an epic life, you have the opportunity to become a master craftswoman. This pillar is your commitment to keep honing your Craft in the world. It is your promise to go beyond the "technical" nature of your profession or training and work to create a thing of beauty—your masterpiece—as a magnificent offering to the world. I love the etymology of "craft," deriving from the Old English *cræft*, meaning "strength or skill." It is also used to describe how a masterly skill can create a life's work of meaningful outcomes. Additionally, craft refers to a hand-built, versatile boat requiring skill to navigate through tricky waters. In the Decade Game, your Craft will be your signature expression of your work in the world.

Committing to mastery in your Craft pillar doesn't mean you need to be in the paid workforce. At this point in her life, based on previous Wall Street jobs, Kim spends more of her time as an investor, mentor, and nonprofit board leader with organizations focusing on girls' empowerment, the environment, justice, and the arts. I love how Kim has named her Craft pillar—**Startist**. How magnificent a name. She has articulated her commitment to use her creativity to start and scale ideas, to create the right conversations which beget the right connections which then turn into the projects, activities, and investments that can change the world. Identifying herself this way has invigorated and enlivened the potential in all her projects. She is now clear on what her real work is when she makes the decision to invest her time and talents in her Craft as a philanthropist, social entrepreneur adviser, and artist.

> "If you go to a master to study and learn the techniques, you diligently follow all the instructions the master puts upon you. But then comes the time for using the rules in your own way and not being bound by them...You are an artist."
>
> —JOSEPH CAMPBELL, *THE POWER OF MYTH*

Your Craft domain can also be the chance to get serious about your hobbies or your leadership in your community. I currently coach several Decade Gamers who have had super successful careers and are now in their late sixties and early seventies.

Betsy was a pioneer in the consumer research industry, retiring after selling the successful firm she built. She had started the firm out of a challenging employment situation, based on a dollar and a prayer, and grew it into a nationally known provider to big brands.

In Chapter 2, we met Stephene, who was educated as a nurse, held important jobs in the federal agency of Health and Human Services, and had run for Congress after her husband, a former congressman, retired.

Both Stephene and Betsy share something in common. Both of their husbands have Alzheimer's disease and have recently been moved into a memory care facility after several years of intense caregiving. At first, the domain of Craft was of no interest to either of them—"Been there done that. It's time for me now" was their instinct.

STAND
I stand for resilience and redemption from hardship

DECADE DESTINATION
Aging gracefully and with strength with a wide circle of dear friends

BETSY'S PLAYHOUSE

Self | Others | Craft | Learn | Legacy

Safe harbour without judgment
Master storyteller
Microfinance
Tasphilas.org*

L1: Get out the door!

L10s

*"girlfriends" in Aramaic

But life isn't over for them as they transition to a new chapter. After identifying her Stand for the power of resilience and promise of redemption to relieve women's hardships, Betsy designed her Decade Game board as a playhouse, not a temple. Her commitment in Craft is to become a Master Storyteller about the journeys of resilient women.

Stephene loved traveling, which she did throughout her career as an international nursing volunteer and a political wife. However, for anyone who has been in politics, you know that the life of a political spouse is never her or his own. Stephene's Stand is for the freedom to make one's own choices to fulfill one's dreams and live life fully with joy and without regrets. Her Craft is a commitment to be a Unique Traveler Without Baggage:

> The Decade Game prompted me to truly think about my life and the direction I want to go to get to a place where I want to be in the next ten years. It directed me to put my thoughts, values, and dreams into writing. Reading and rereading them made my dreams for the next decade seem doable. Having the game to play moving forward, seeing my progress, having the fun of actually doing things I want to do, and changing it up as I go because I can is wonderful to look forward to. As they say: you can't get there from here, but you can get here from there!

Many of the women who play the Decade Game are deep in the middle of their earning years in their thirties to fifties, consumed by their jobs and working to overdeliver for their paycheck as they compete in what is still a man's world. Their "jobs" both define them and confine them. Their traditional job titles, be it VP of Sales or Human Resources Director, don't come close to identifying or valuing their unique talents and gifts that have been honed by exceeding expectations in their simultaneous jobs of being a leader at home and in their communities.

Tanya is a case in point. A lawyer by training, Tanya is in her late forties and the deputy general counsel for a major company. She will be in the "paid" workforce for decades to come, most likely being paid to do lawyer-like projects. Her Craft aspiration doesn't reflect her technical training. It is a manifestation of what her unique gifts are that can be transformational in any setting. Here are the highlights of her game board:

Tanya's Stand: *I stand for the power of genuine curiosity to create a world of empathy and empowerment where every individual can live their fullest life, valued for who they are.*

Tanya's Decade Destination: *To be known as an Irrepressible Puzzler and Passionate Conductor Bringing People Together to Solve Problems and Create Harmony.*

Given this directive, she named her work of Craft as **Cathedral Builder.** Her vision is to build a unique mastery in her ability to grasp the big picture, bring together diverse opinions to solve multidimensional problems, and inspire people to learn, be their best, and dream big. Tanya has envisioned her Level 10 in Craft, that iconic view of what mastery would look like in ten years, as being a "celebrated executive recognized for driving results through inclusion and diversity, a sought-after speaker and board member, and a zealous and effective advocate for women in the corporate world." And yes, still a lawyer by training. She reflected on it this way:

Confronting professional and personal choices that will, in fact, define my next decade and beyond, the Decade Game reminded me that I am the author of my own epic-ness, that if I can dream it, I can be it.

Two decades ago, I had an insight about Craft. Employees need the freedom to love what they do and the way they do it if they are going to be fully engaged. They also need to be valued and celebrated for their unique gifts, which contribute to group genius. Otherwise, they might quit but still stay on the job. This became clear to me at a partners' meeting that EY held every three years for the 4,000-plus partners in North America. We had a rotating chairmanship, and at one of the partners' meetings in 2000, our chairman-elect asked an important question to everyone as we considered the strategy for the next decade: "What would we do differently if all our people were volunteers?"

I have built many teams in my corporate tenure, and I have taken this question seriously. The most creative people who work for you are, in essence, volunteers, no matter what you pay them. The greatest and most untapped technology in the world is a human being's capacity and desire to creatively solve problems. To unleash human potential, people need to contribute much more than their technical skills. They're learning how to contribute their energy, hope, vulnerability, love, and the quality of their presence in service of what they are most passionate about. Mission-driven companies deliver on their promise when they can engage the epic spirit and talents of their employees.

In the epic game of your life, your decade destination is your mission for the next decade. Your Self and Others pillars guide your "human being-ness." The Craft pillar guides your "human doing-ness." Done well, you might be temporarily out of a project or product in Craft, but never out of a job. And as importantly, as expressed by the last line in this beautiful poem *The Craftsman*, written by the African American poet Marcus Christian in middle of the twentieth century in New Orleans..."He who creates true beauty ever lives."

The Craftsman

I ply with all the cunning of my art
This little thing, and with consummate care
I fashion it—so that when I depart,
Those who come after me shall find it fair
And beautiful. It must be free of flaws—
Pointing no laborings of weary hands;
And there must be no flouting of the laws
Of beauty—as the artist understands.
Through passion, yearnings infinite—yet dumb—
I lift you from the depths of my own mind
And gild you with my soul's white heat to plumb
The souls of future men. I leave behind
This thing that in return this solace gives:
"He who creates true beauty ever lives."

—Marcus B. Christian[1]

1 Marcus B. Christian, "The Craftsman" from *The Poetry of the Negro 1746–1970.* Copyright © 1970 by Marcus B. Christian. Reprinted by permission of University of New Orleans, Marcus B. Christian Papers, Earl K. Long Library.

Getting Started: Naming Your Craft Pillar

Naming this pillar should be fun and illuminate a game-changing capability or capacity that isn't mainstream today but will be an important agent of transformation. Maybe your Craft is to help build a capability that doesn't exist today but will be essential to transform the current state of technology, or healthcare, or education, or communities. After all, many of the cool job descriptions today did not exist a decade ago. Social media influencer, driverless car engineer, telemedicine expert, and podcast producer were figments of imagination in 2010. Your title for this pillar could be a derivation of the outrageous job description you gave yourself in your Mad Lib destination.

Your Craft represents how you choose to offer and package your unique skills, talents, techniques, knowledge, and gifts as your signature "work" in the world—be it in the business, nonprofit, government, or civic sectors. It reflects your commitment to be a master craftsman in your field of interest—a master that can inspire others and can be counted on to bring "a thing of beauty" into the world. You name the pillar for the unique way you will have an impact in your chosen field.

Naming Convention: Think about your Craft pillar as if you, as the Master craftswoman, were your own company or organization. You are the CEO—Chief Experience Officer. And you have a calling card that would clearly telegraph what kind of unique masterpieces people would "hire" you for.

Why and for what would people hire you above all others? You hire me because I am _____.

To give you more ideas, here are examples of how participants in a recent Decade Game Master Class named their Craft pillar on their game board. Note that these titles don't deal with the technical nature of the profession—lawyer, doctor, consultant, coach, engineer—but rather, the specific quality of presence, intentional impact, and innovativeness these Decade Gamers are bringing to their Craft.

- Innovative Designer of Education
- Modern-day Mystic and Archeologist of the Divine
- Wizard of Oz (for the strategic thinking that I bring to my industry)
- Anthropologist of the Future.
- "Hat Trick" Warrior (Mind, Body, and Spirit)
- Lifetime Cruise Director in Preventive Care and Wellbeing
- Workplace Shaman Inspiring the Sacred in Work
- Intuitive Healer of Grief and Loss
- Creator of Life-Giving Spaces
- Master Designer/Facilitator/Un-locker of Group Genius
- A True Nature Guide
- Master Leadership Choreographer

Questions to Consider.

1. When you think about your Stand and your decade destination, what is the "doing" that is necessary for this field of endeavor? What would we call the new world experts?

2. Who is a game changer today in this field, and what is the game they're trying to shift?

3. What is the core knowledge or approach that currently doesn't exist that will be essential to change the game?

4. What is the particular industry/sector (i.e., healthcare, entertainment, education, government, technology) where you would love to devote 10,000 hours to become a master?

Rules of the Game:
Be totally present in the now and
totally ready for the future.

Chapter 9

Learning

A Journey of Unknowing

Mary and I could have been separated at birth, although she is more than a decade younger than me. We were both executive women on Wall Street at a time when senior women were few and far between. Although I was an expert in multi-billion-dollar mergers, acquisitions, and complex financings, Mary navigated a double whammy as an expert in a field that was even more unusual for women—information technology. She started her career as a coder and worked her way up to top jobs at a global investment bank while raising her daughter as a single mother. After a stint leading the information technology support team for the Asia Pacific region living in Japan, Mary became the global chief technology officer at the company.

Mary is unflappable, super smart, of the highest integrity, and fearless. These characteristics allowed her to both flourish and retain her soul in what is sometimes a soulless industry. When I met Mary, she had just retired from her firm and joined me on the Board of Auburn Theological Seminary. Auburn is a 200-year-old seminary in New York City whose mission is to help equip bold and resilient leaders of faith and moral courage to trouble the waters and heal the world.

Auburn was a perfect place for Mary's leadership. Throughout her life, she has always chosen the pathway of moral courage, working to promote justice and equity. Having retired, and her only daughter launched in her career trajectory to become an ordained chaplain, Mary was ready for her next decade. From her roots growing up in Iowa, Mary decided to leave the urban landscape of New York and New Jersey and settle permanently in Montana. Everything in her life was up for redesign. Where she lived, how she worked, a new community, and new projects. Knowing her accomplishments and intentions so far, I was confident Mary would be as dedicated to this next decade as she has been in her life up to now.

Mary was able to identify her Stand more quickly than many Decade Gamers. I have a hypothesis about this. Many of the women I know who personally thrive while working in the money-obsessed, workaholic culture of Wall Street are able to do so because they are more clearly connected to their real purpose—which is not money. Mary, like me, had chosen to learn how to get power, keep power, and use that power to make a difference. Her colleagues could count on Mary to be a voice of moral leadership in her firm, using her power on behalf of women and historically underrepresented groups at the company. She also leveraged her power and influence externally in her philanthropic contributions to society.

Mary's Stand: *Every person experiences inclusive, thriving, just, vibrant communities of caring and connectedness so that they are filled with the richness of life.*

Mary's Decade Destination: *I will be known as an Innovator, Conscious Collaborator, and Builder of Transformative Communities.*

This pillar is the domain of Learning, and it can be confusing. All the pillars are infused with specific learning in doing the work of self, relatedness, craft, and contribution. For Mary, transplanting herself from thirty years on Wall Street to Absarokee, Montana, would require learning across the board. In Self, her work is to shift her own inner constitution of self-reliance and belief in the story of aloneness to "A Love Fest" anchored by practices of self-love. Mary named her Others pillar "The Naturalist" to focus on the energy of becoming an "earth person," experiencing her connectedness with Mother Earth and grounding her relationships with loved ones. Her Craft work is to become a "Coalition Builder" and a contributing member and beloved elder of the Absarokee community. For Mary, the goal of these three connected games within the overall Decade Game is to help "hospice the Western myth of rugged individualism and honor the other part of the pioneer story of community support and collaboration combined with indigenous wisdom." Lots of learning in each of those pillars.

Why do we need a separate pillar of 10,000 hours for Learning? The learnings embedded with the other domains are driven by a sense of what winning looks like to build mastery as expressed in both the name and Level 10s of your Self, Others, and Craft pillars. For example, in Self, you might have decided on specific learning objectives to achieve a new level in your spiritual and physical health through meditation and exercise. In Others, you have very specific relationships in mind and might want to learn more about trauma, co-dependency, and internal family systems to achieve the breakthroughs you are longing for. In Craft, there might be a specific industry, technology, or product category that you want to become an expert in.

This domain invites in the love of learning for Learning's sake. It gives you permission to be on a journey of awe, wonder, and adventure as a core part of your job. By committing to a journey of discovery, you are also committing to a journey of unlearning. Creating the new stories for the most epic decade yet requires you to unwind the patterns and interpretations of how the world works and open new vistas of possibilities.

In the challenging years of 2020 and 2021, as we faced racial injustice, climate change, and the pandemic, many of the Decade Gamers I work with wanted their journey of unknowing to help "decolonize" their minds and break free of their conditioning about the unquestioned patterns of being and doing that lock in the status quo. The interesting thing about patterns is that they need all their parts to be able to continue. Changing just one piece of the pattern changes the whole system.

This pillar gives you the luxury of time and space to learn with abandon about areas you are passionate about. Creating the opportunity for continuous learning is a precondition for innovation and creativity. It turns out that most innovations happen on the conjoined border of what is known in two distinct fields. A great example of this today is Apple. What started as a computer company has now transformed the watch, camera, music, and entertainment industries. By learning what was happening in other industries, Apple continued to transform its own industry. How apt that their slogan is "Think different."

To have a decade of metamorphosis, we are imagining a future for ourselves that does not yet exist. We are also striving to be practical innovators, living in the space of possibilities, not improbabilities, with actions that can be taken immediately (our tiny mighties). Great designers call this liminal space "the magic of the adjacent possible." It is the combination of these knowns that, when combined with the unknowns, creates the chance of something totally new.

In the same way that the Self and Others are interrelated, this pillar is closely related to your Craft domain. Learning is creativity from the outside in. As a student of the world, you are learning weirdly and wildly about a variety of topics, capturing external knowledge and bringing it into your Craft. Creativity is learning from the inside out. As a "master," you are then able to export your innovations from your Craft to spur the learning of others.

STAND
I stand for courageous
leaders trusting their magic, leaning into
the mystery, and mobilizing others for transformation

DECADE DESTINATION
Organizational Shaman Inspiring Humans to Live Epic Lives

Craft

Decade Game is
global practice
for women

I am
Sensei

Create
Imaginal Labs

Learning

Wisdom Keeper
with energy
medicine
harmonizing
sacred masculine
and feminine in
action

Shamanic
Wisdom

Honeymoon
Climb Kilimanjaro

In my current sixty to seventy Decade Game, my Learning pillar has been one of the biggest engines of my decade design. At sixty, having reached mandatory retirement as a management consultant, I set my game for seventy with a decade destination "to be known as an Organizational Shaman Inspiring Humans to Lead Epic Lives." A challenging and exciting decade destination. Except for the fact that I had never met a shaman. I named my Learning pillar "Shamanic Wisdom." This gave me permission to say "yes" to a magnificent smorgasbord of new ideas: indigenous wisdom, the natural world, magic, ritual and ceremony, cognition, plant medicine, and sacred feminine energy. It also set me on a journey to unlearn the blind spots of the consumer-focused, colonial, modern world that I was born into. From choosing to climb Kilimanjaro, as one of my early Level 1 tiny mighties, to annual deep immersions in the

Amazon rain forest, I have been seeking out shamans ever since to learn from. This Learning and "unlearning" journey has shifted everything for me. I am softer, less judgmental, and more trusting, having tapped deeply into the sacred feminine knowing that is available to all of us. It has also been a huge contributor to my Craft of being a Sensei for Women's Leadership.

Mary's name for her Learning pillar is "Art and Spirit." It seemed like a wonderful antidote to three decades of math and science to now be able to invest 10,000 hours in subjects that she hadn't had time for previously. Mary's desire to build community, connect to nature, slow down her life, and find deeper richness required her to infuse her journey with art and spirit. She was already an accomplished amateur astrologist, making charts for all her friends. When trying to imagine what this domain of Learning could encompass, I suggested designing an imaginary PhD where she could combine all the electives that would be fun to study, resulting in an honorary degree of her own naming. Some of the electives Mary imagined that could enhance this Learning journey included photography, beading, spiritual rejuvenation, consciousness, and the spiritual underpinnings of transformation.

I love Mary's story of what happened next. She had been keeping her eye out for potential businesses to invest in. She knew from her Decade Game that part of becoming a beloved elder in her town could include becoming a local business owner. A hardware store was available. Also, a dry goods store. But these options did not touch her heart. Then one day, she was driving down the Main Street of Absarokee and passed by a small quilting store with a FOR SALE sign in the window. It was a "Eureka!" moment. Given her decade destination of Builder of Beloved Community, she immediately had visions of quilting bees with circles of women quilting together, sharing patches of material, and creating designs picturing forms of nature.

Two months later, Mary was the proud owner of the Cloud Nine Quilts. The store is a community gathering place for women. Mary is creating learning opportunities by having people teach classes in different types of quilting. The store has never had an online presence, and Mary is using her expertise from her many years in information technology to create that potential channel for social media, communal learning, and revenue for the quilters. Mary also has a separate building on her ranch and has plans to convert it into an art and retreat center for women. Mary is learning to become a master quilter as well as a small business entrepreneur. So much Learning in the first year into her Decade Game, a great set of Level 1 "tiny mighties."

Getting Started: Naming Your Learning Pillar

Your domain of Learning represents the journey of discovery—learning and unlearning—for the pure curiosity and joy of it. Learning outside your "chosen field" is the foundation for creativity and innovation IN your chosen field. It is the conduit for new insights, perspectives, and foresight. This pillar also allows you to say "yes" to new experiences and cool adventures that will give you revelation, relaxation, and rejuvenation.

Review your Stand as well as your decade journal entry to think about all the things you want to learn and experience in the world.

Naming Convention: Start by listing all the required and elective courses of the experiences you want to have and the people/places you want to learn from in your imagined curriculum and fieldwork. Then name the title of your imagined PhD program or dissertation that describes your newfound mastery.

What/why/how do people learn from me? I have a PhD in _____.

Here are fun examples of recent Decade Gamer's PhDs that might prompt your ideas of a Learning journey worth a 10,000-hour investment:

- PhD in Work Hard and Play Hard
- PhD in Mysticism
- PhD in Ecosystem Interdependence
- PhD in "Sacred Work"
- PhD in Golf (one of my favorites from someone who is tired of the grind)
- PhD in Compromise Through Gardening
- PhD in Infinite Imagination
- PhD in Male Motivation
- PhD in How Change Happens for individuals, communities, organizations, and institutions
- PhD in Women's Liberation and Power
- PhD in Self Work and Self-Discovery Tools
- PhD in Professional Encouragement

Questions to Consider

1. What topic has always intrigued you that could be a game-changer for the future direction of society?

2. If you could have the coolest "elective" PhD, what would you want to learn?

3. What are examples of some of the "courses" that would be part of that Learning curriculum? Who are the current masters/authors/experts in the field?

4. How might that topic/subject be helpful to your overall Decade Game Stand and destination?

Rules of the Game:
When in Rome, do as the Romanians do.

Chapter 10

Contribution

You are the Gift that keeps on giving

In describing Lynne Twist, I like to say that she is an angel having a human experience. Lynne is a role model for so many people. She is the epitome of someone living a committed life. As described in her memoir and best-selling book *The Soul of Money,* Lynne has lived a life of meaning and purpose that has taken her to the slums of Calcutta working with Mother Teresa, to the famine-ravaged and war-torn countries of Africa, and to the pristine forests of the Amazon River basin working closely to empower indigenous leaders in their battles to protect the lungs of the world. She is a

remarkable pro-activist and possibilist, a compelling fund-
raiser, a sage counselor, a devoted mother and grandmother,
an adoring spouse, and a dear friend. It is from Lynne that I
learned the power of a Stand.

When we drafted her Decade Game board in 2016, it was
hard for Lynne to name her Stand's essence, given all her
many initiatives, projects, and causes. Here are just a few.
She is the co-founder of The Pachamama Alliance, whose
mission is to bring forth an environmentally sustainable,
socially just, spiritually fulfilling human presence on the
planet. Lynne is the founder of The Soul of Money Institute,
dedicated to creating a context of sufficiency, responsibility,
and integrity for individuals and organizations in their relationship with money. She also serves as a strategic adviser to
the women who have won the Nobel Peace Prize through the
Nobel Women's Initiative. What was the narrative tapestry
that weaves together all these world-changing endeavors with
Lynne's unique magic? This is where we landed. Anyone who
has been in Lynne's presence feels the illuminating power of
her love—and they are transformed by it to make a difference
with their life.

Lynne's Stand:

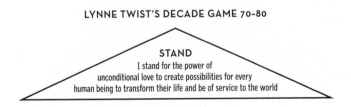

LYNNE TWIST'S DECADE GAME 70-80

STAND
I stand for the power of
unconditional love to create possibilities for every
human being to transform their life and be of service to the world

We also had a great time coming up with her new decade destination. It was challenging to think about what the next evolutionary leap for Lynne could be, given how epic her work has been to date. What does future mastery look like for an angel? The answer came to us like a lightning bolt. Lynne's eyes began to sparkle, and we knew we had it.

Lynne's Decade Destination:

DESTINATION
The Fairy Godmother of mythic mindsets and movements that transform the world

---

Lynne is not done being of service. She came of age as a disciple of Buckminster Fuller, the great American architect, systems theorist, author, designer, inventor, and futurist, and Werner Erhard, founder of the EST training and renowned contributor to the human growth potential movement. From her work on climate change, protection of the rain forest, women's empowerment, racial justice, conscious capitalism, and reallocation of the world's resources, she believes the essential work of women is to lead the way to hospice the old systems in the world and midwife the new. She wants to do her part in igniting the power of the Sophia Century where women take their rightful role with men to put the world in balance.

The Contribution pillar is what I call "a tricky bit" given that the entire Decade Game is a contribution to yourself, the people you love, your stated profession, and to society. Here is the distinction. The first four pillars are the commitment to grow *YOUR* mastery over the next ten years in the domains of Self, Others, and "the collective"—your engagement with the outside world. This pillar is about freely donating the gifts of your mastery to other masters who are committed to a similar Stand as you. Lynne has had a personal relationship with others who also stand for the power of unconditional love to transform lives. Mother Teresa, Archbishop Desmond Tutu, Jane Goodall, to name a few. Yet her specific superpowers, presence, and mastery, freely given to them, have been great gifts that have contributed to their impact.

In this domain, you are not attached to any outcomes other than the magical possibilities that are generated when you freely give your hard-won gifts to other masters for an epic purpose, requiring no promises in return. You are also playing a much longer game here. Given this pillar's direct connection to your Stand—your life's work and your legacy— you don't feel the same pressure as in the other domains to see specific results even in your lifetime. You are in it to contribute to progress. You have been nourished by the harvest of the fruits of the labors of others who came before us. And you are planting the seeds for the work of future generations. This open-ended, unbound commitment is both liberating and liberated from the pressure of time and outcomes.

"You don't want modesty, you want humility. Humility comes from inside out. It says someone was here before me and I'm here because I've been paid for. I have something to do and I will do that because I'm paying for someone else who has yet to come."

—MAYA ANGELOU

I learned this by sitting on boards of nonprofit organizations. By not having a title, specific job responsibilities, or a contract that kept me in my own box of "expertise," I learned the full impact of what I know and how I show up. Whether learned in my personal journey, in my family system, or in honing my Craft, I was able to combine all this knowing and freely give it as a gift to amazing organizations, causes, and leaders who share my vision for how the world gets better. You never know what seeds will take root. But you can be assured that your hard-earned and intentional mastery, committed consistently over a decade combined with theirs, will contribute to group genius and miracles.

You can think about the work of Contribution this way. It could signal a critical issue that breaks your heart and is keeping the world from working, e.g., climate change, women and girls' empowerment, flourishing of all sentient beings, resolving conflict, economic security, etc. Or it could be "leader-based" to support the journey of specific leaders (whom you trust as "Jedi Masters") and their organizations across a range of issues. Or it could be geographically focused, like the transformation and well-being of the continent of Africa or supporting indigenous societies. Regardless of your focus, these organizations, issue areas, and leaders need your magic.

My Contribution pillar is leader-based, given that my Stand is that the world gets better when courageous leaders find their magic. My pillar is entitled "Courageous Leaders" and guides me to seek out the transformational leaders who are bringing their magic into the world and need my magic to make their greatest contributions. I am both their teacher and their disciple, and they say the same about me. It is this intention that brought me to the feet and heart of Lynne.

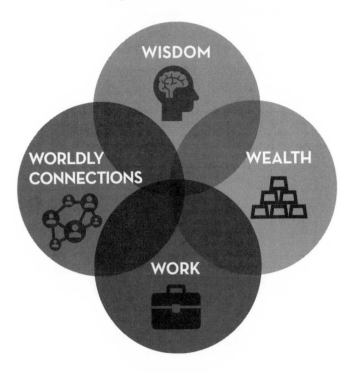

A simple way to think about this is that the Contribution pillar is your philanthropic domain. But it is so much more. You are committing to be "all in" with your 10,000 hours and everything else you have to offer. As the chief investment officer of all your gifts, it is the compounded impact of your "four Ws"—your wealth, your wisdom, your work, and your worldly connections—that you are looking to invest.

Lynne named her Contribution pillar "Shapeshifters.org" with a commitment to invest her "four Ws" in projects that will make a difference at the system level. Perfect for the "fairy godmother of mythic mindsets and movements"! For someone who was always "of service" to anyone who asked, this declaration helped Lynne focus and prioritize her "yes" to the organizations and leaders who have a chance of

moving the dial for the entire planet. At the young age of seventy, Lynne wants to make sure that her next decade will be the most impactful of her life.

Since creating her game board five years ago, she has doubled down on her gifts of mastery to organizations like The Fetzer Institute, which has a 500-year commitment to build the spiritual foundation for a more loving world; The Nobel Women's Initiative, an advocacy organization created to support women's groups around the world in campaigning for justice, peace, and equality; and the Sacred Headwaters project, a new multidecade, multibillion-dollar global initiative to permanently protect the Amazon rain forest.

Let's look at Lynne's entire game board. It is clear that Lynne is all about contribution, even when she is sleeping. She has identified her own work of growing in mastery in the first four pillars of Self, Others, Craft, and Learning. All to the benefit of what gifts she brings to other masters who are Shape Shifters.

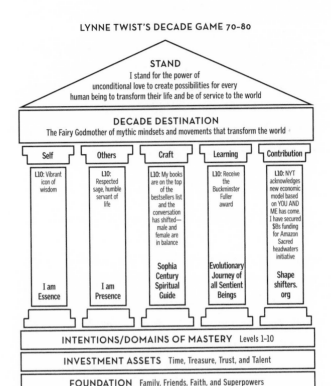

LYNNE TWIST'S DECADE GAME 70-80

STAND
I stand for the power of
unconditional love to create possibilities for every
human being to transform their life and be of service to the world

DECADE DESTINATION
The Fairy Godmother of mythic mindsets and movements that transform the world

Self	Others	Craft	Learning	Contribution
L10: Vibrant icon of wisdom	L10: Respected sage, humble servant of life	L10: My books are on the top of the bestsellers list and the conversation has shifted— male and female are in balance	L10: Receive the Buckminster Fuller award	L10: NYT acknowledges new economic model based on YOU AND ME has come. I have secured $Bs funding for Amazon Sacred headwaters initiative
I am Essence	I am Presence	Sophia Century Spiritual Guide	Evolutionary Journey of all Sentient Beings	Shape shifters. org

INTENTIONS/DOMAINS OF MASTERY   Levels 1–10

INVESTMENT ASSETS   Time, Treasure, Trust, and Talent

FOUNDATION   Family, Friends, Faith, and Superpowers

Getting Started: Naming Your Contribution Pillar

Your Contribution pillar represents where you are "all in"
with your wealth, wisdom, work, and worldly connections
(the "four Ws") in a domain that will be the "major" of your
philanthropic focus for the decade. It will be an area where
other masters sharing a similar Stand need your gifts to
support their mastery. This pillar could include different
organizations and specific areas over the decade, but they
will have a coherent through line that is consistent with your
Stand. Broad domain examples could include environment,

women's and/or girls' empowerment, marginalized communities, healthcare, inequality, good governance, etc.

Naming Convention: This domain of mastery is most easily named by giving it the title of your imagined granting foundation or nonprofit that would reflect and telegraph to "grantees" the areas you are committed to invest in.

In what sector/area can people count on your "4W" philanthropy? "You can count on me for supporting _____."

Here are some of the fantastic domain titles from recent Decade Game participants. Just imagine the unmet needs in the world that are longing to be addressed where the gifts of mastery offered by these remarkable women, their four Ws, would be well invested.

- Boysclubbulldozer.org
- Accelerator of Educators and Mystics.org
- Tasphilas.org (means "girlfriends" in Aramaic)
- Unleashing Silence into Greatness.org
- What Would Greta Do.org
- Olive Branch.org
- CommunityTable.org
- Authentic Bridge.org
- Joyful Equity Connectors.org
- Find Your Story.com
- I got Your back.org
- infinite possibilities.org
- Leaders for modern growth.org

- A Re-imagined World.org
- Getting Them There.org
- thebiggerpicture.org
- The Emancipation Platform.org

Questions to consider

1. What is the "through line" that defines your historical philanthropic and community activities?

2. What are two "issue" areas that capture your greatest longing for the world that are connected closely to your Stand?

3. What organizations or causes can count on you for your talents and treasures?

4. What could you do with your four Ws in the next twelve months to up-level your impact?

Rules of the Game:
Practice thoughtful wishing
instead of wishful thinking

Section IV

Power, on Purpose

The Women's Hour

Not for herself! Though sweet the air of freedom;
Not for herself! The dear the new-born power;
But for the Child who needs a nobler Mother,
For the Whole People needing One another,
Comes Woman to her Hour.

—CHARLOTTE PERKINS GILMAN,
(novelist, essayist, and prominent
suffragette) published in 1912

Chapter 11

Sisterhood Is an Epic Multiplayer Game

For what purpose do women need power? Why are we so keen to achieve gender parity at the kitchen and board room tables? Why are we not there yet, one hundred years after women achieved the vote? Why am I not there yet, no matter how hard I have worked for it? The missing ingredient is sisterhood.

In 2002, I transferred from a national assignment at EY to the NY Metro regional office, which included over 5,000 people in NYC, Connecticut, and NJ. Although we were close to gender parity for all staff employees, only about twenty partners, representing less than 10 percent of the regional partnership, were women. And the women partners weren't playing nice with each other. Being the new shiny object (and one of the oldest) in the mix, our office managing partner asked me to see what I could do. I had a lot of compassion for the women partners. I had been at EY for a decade, having been hired in as a partner. I knew how hard my women partners were working, managing all their personal and professional obligations.

A little background is helpful here. In the mid-1990s, EY began to get serious about the path toward gender equity. Even then, over 50 percent of college graduates were women, and it was becoming evident that trend would continue. At that time, only 3 percent of our partners nationally were women. We did a detailed study to illuminate the biggest hurdles that were holding women back and decided to work on the following:

- Strengthen women's internal networks
- Strengthen women's external networks
- Mentoring
- Improve conditions and incentives for work/life balance
- Create more flexible work arrangements

We assigned the Human Resources department the primary responsibility for the latter two levers and gave the women themselves the job of mentoring and strengthening women's networks. The core questions we had to address were this: "Why don't women, who are such natural connectors, have strong networks that facilitate relationship development, business acumen, and career success?" and "Why aren't we taking care of each other?" Our exploration yielded key insights:

- Women were more comfortable relating to each other around common "personal" experiences as well as shared "on the job" emotions of frustration, annoyances, anxieties, and "little victories." This perception fed a suspicion in our dominant male culture that women's networks were just "coffee klatches," informal gatherings that didn't pertain to real work.
- Women didn't want to be guilty by association and perceived as not as committed to the organization's goals as the men. We were reluctant to build our own version of "the old boys' network."
- Women build their networks by developing authentic relationships and are hesitant to impose on their friendships by moving into a "transactional, self-serving" sphere to advance business prospects. This hesitancy kept women from identifying and supporting each other in their career ambitions and goals.
- Networking felt so "political" and "self-serving." Women wanted none of that. Therefore, the "Good Girls" were leaking power in their solo journey to fit in and win a game that was rigged against them.

- As to mentoring others, although we wanted to, we were too busy figuring it out for ourselves and then needed to get home to take up our other full-time job.

TRI-STATE PWN STRATEGY AND MISSION

Tri-State PWN Mission	Tri-State PWN Goals	Key Areas of Networking Focus
Build our women's confidence, skills, leadership opportunities, and internal and external networks—leading to satisfying careers and increased levels of success for our women and the Firm.	• Women "at the table" • Friends at work • Appreciating and leveraging our women's unique skills and talents	• Internal development • Community development • External development

Aware of these challenges, I was excited to gather with my women partners and help figure out how we could play together more effectively and uplift our career trajectory. I set one condition before I agreed to take this on. Our work had to be considered part of our job responsibilities and not something we would do "in our spare time." In our initial meeting, we were able to reframe what game was worth playing together, and the Tri-State Professional Women's Network ("PWN") was born. It was authorized as a project that the women partners who took a leadership role could devote up to 10 percent of our time, on average. We moved the goalpost of success past our own careers to a focus on helping other women step into their power and purpose with the following mission: build our women's confidence, skills, leadership opportunities, and internal and external networks—leading to satisfying careers and increased levels of success for our women and the firm. The commitment to sisterhood was the game worth playing to win. In the decade after its inception, the PWN became a beloved part of women's EY experience. We won external awards for the model and marked many achievements in the following areas:

- Flexibility of work schedules for our women professionals
- Retention improvement at every level
- Percentage of women in the partnership
- Percentage of women serving key accounts
- Increased percentage of new partners that are women
- Number of women in the "partner pipeline"
- Number of PWN participants
- Improving People Survey Scores ("Have a best friend at work")

The experience taught me that it's not enough for individual women to play their own Decade Game to rediscover their destiny. Women need to play together for good. When women stop competing, comparing, and criticizing each other and, instead, stand for each other's power, beauty, ambitions, vulnerabilities, and accomplishments, the world changes. Divide and be conquered is a game that favors those already in power.

Women have the choice to become new role models and heroines for each other. The #MeToo moment was critical to our future, but it is not sufficient. The stories finally being told are embedded in the old archetypes of men as perpetrators and women as victims. In that story, every actor has character flaws that resound with shame and pain, not possibilities. It's time for a new narrative that women can and must champion.

Our world is crying out for this new sisterhood to address the world's challenges—war, climate change, poverty, inequality, injustice. At a time when we have four generations of women active in society, the world is pregnant with possibilities for transformation. We have the power to change the falsehood that women don't play well together. In fact, we are at our best when we play together in good times and in bad. We are the connective tissue that makes the world work. And now we are at an unprecedented pivotal epoch in history when, for the first time, we have the connectivity to be a global sisterhood, weaving together our superpowers and feminine knowing to become, as Campbell predicted, the "ancestors of an age to come."

I am sure that each of you reading this book has worked hard for a long time to empower yourself and others. Here is what I am clear about. You can't do this on your own. It's too hard. Even though we have been at this for almost a century, progress is still too slow. But we can do this together by playing a multiplayer game that enables the next evolutionary leap for women's contribution to the world.

As you read in the foreword, Lynne calls our time "The Sophia Century," when women will take their rightful role in full, equal partnership with men and the feminine and masculine energies in each of us will come into right relationship so that humanity will soar. In one of the Remarkable Women's Journey cohorts that I co-lead with Lynne, the participants combined their Stands into a communal Decade Game that reflects their collective sisterhood as one body. Listen to their superpowers and imagine the ripple effects over a lifetime of these talents unleashed into the world.

A Communal Decade Game of Sisterhood

- I see those who are invisible.
- I stay in the energy of love and don't move into fear.
- I have a bionic ear so we can listen in a new way.
- I communicate in many dimensions synthesized.
- I have infinite capacity to love and understand and be with everything just as it is in the world.
- I trust children and see them as sovereign and committed expressing that in all places.
- I hold space for authentic and deep connection.
- I have a powerful connection with the divine that manifests all the right places.
- I speak truth to unlock potential access and reverence for my own divinity.
- I practice righteous endurance through adversity.
- I connect people because I see who they are.
- I believe in the healing of restorative love.
- I can be with things as they are and as they are not.
- I see the magic in others and help them trust that magic.

It is not a new concept that energized sisterhood can bring about epic change. Did you know that Mother's Day, the "hallmark" holiday that we now celebrate in the US on the first Sunday in May, had a very different birth purpose? This holiday had its origins in the heart and pen of Juliet Ward Howe, the famous lyricist of the "Battle Hymn of the Republic" written during the Civil War. While an ardent supporter of the fight to end slavery and keep the Union together, she was sickened by the carnage of the Civil War. In 1870, appalled by the outbreak of the Franco-Prussian War and the clamoring of young men to go fight overseas, she declared a Mothers' Day Proclamation for Peace and had it translated into French, Spanish, Italian, German, and Swedish and disseminated internationally. Hear her words:

> Arise arise…great congress of women of all nation-alities who have hearts, whether your baptism be of water or of tears…We will not have great questions decided by irrelevant agencies…and our children shall not be taken from us to unlearn all that we have been able to teach them of charity, mercy, and patience…We women of one country will be too tender to those of another country to allow our sons to be trained to injure theirs…Let women now leave all that may be left of home for a great and earnest day of counsel with each other as to the means whereby the great human family can live in peace, each bearing after his time the sacred impress not of Caesar but of God.

She ended her proclamation by declaring…

In the name of womanhood and humanity, I earnestly ask that a general congress of women without limit of nationality be appointed and held at some place deemed most convenient and at the earliest period consistent with its objects, to promote the alliance of the different nationalities, the amicable settlement of international questions, the great and general interests of peace.

Two years later, in 1872, Howe went to London to spread her message, and when an established peace organization there would not let her speak because of her gender, she hired her own hall to conduct her meeting.

So here we are. One hundred and fifty years later, as we come out of the years of the 2020–2021 Pandemic Great Pause, "women of all nationalities who have hearts, whether your baptism be of water or of tears" are pondering the great question of the twenty-first century, "How can the human family live in peace with each other and the natural world?"

The answer to this question falls on each of us to respond in our unique way, drawing on our authentic gifts. We are being called on to choose to be brave, to be courageous, and to be, yes, EPIC! We women are all mothers at heart, be it for our own children or all children, known and unknown. We have a deep intergenerational knowing, passed on genetically, culturally, biologically, and psychologically. We are the birthers, the nurturers, and the mourners. We feel the urgent call to hospice the old soul-crushing systems and midwife the life-giving systems of the future. We have epic work to do.

Whether you are twenty-eight or eighty-eight, we have a great responsibility to "Arise Arise" and leverage our untapped power to gain decision rights to shape a better future. Each of us has the potential to be heroines in our time, to speak the truth, to draw on the collective strength of sisterhood, to inspire others to cross the man-made boundaries that divide us from our essential selves and each other. We have the power to birth the healthy future that our great-great-grandchildren will thank us for. To fulfill our destiny, we need to pen our own stories about what it means to be a woman—a sister to each other, a mother to all children, a leader, a citizen of moral courage. Instead of living in stories that we were written into, women can begin seizing control of the sagas we want to live into. We can support each other to muster the courage to imagine new plots, rewrite narratives, and heal the character flaws that hold us back.

This call to women of the twenty-first century was best said by my friend, the magical Sikh activist, lawyer, and founder of Revolutionary Love, Valarie Kaur, in a prayer breakfast in Washington on the eve of the 2017 presidential inauguration:

> What if this darkness is not the darkness of the
> tomb, but the darkness of the womb?…What if all
> of our grandfathers and grandmothers are stand-
> ing behind now?…What if they are whispering in
> our ears "You are brave"? What if this is our nation's

greatest transition…What does the midwife tell us to do? Breathe. And then, Push. Because if we don't push, we will die…Tonight we will breathe. Tomorrow we will labor…through love and your revolutionary love is the magic we will show our children.

We do this not just for us. Twenty-first century heroines know that today's heroes are suffering as well. So much has been placed on their shoulders. From early ages, reinforced by society's hero stories, they also have had to give up parts of their essential nature—their feminine energy—for the good of family and society. Or so they were told. I have four sons, a son-in law, two grandsons, a wonderful husband, and many male colleagues. Their tears and pain, the full measure of their humanity, are buried deep within. By discovering our power and unleashing it in each decade, we can liberate them as well.

Truly, an epic multiplayer game worth the money.

Rules of the Game: An epic life is an off-road journey

Chapter 12

Game On

The history of your EPIC! future begins today. Every day you can discover meaning for yourself and create meaning for others if you are playing your game, by your rules, on purpose, for a purpose greater than yourself.

We have come a long way since the Great Man Theory, developed by the Scottish philosopher Thomas Carlyle in the nineteenth century in his 1841 book, *On Heroes, Hero-Worship, and The Heroic in History*. Since then, there have been countervailing arguments on which theory of history is most true. Do great men make history? Or does history make great men?

Once again, these male historians have gotten this 100 percent half right. When women embrace their epic-ness, requiring the harmonization of their masculine and feminine energies of being and doing, the truth is "yes, and."

This insight became clearer to me when I participated in *Fortune*'s Most Powerful Women's ("MPW") conference a decade ago. This conference was held every year follow-ing the publication of *Fortune*'s cover story of the 50 Most Powerful Women in business. The MPW conference convenes the most prominent women in the Fortune 500 and leaders from the world of politics, the arts, and NGOs. At the gath-ering, participants choose from a variety of workshops that supplement the plenary sessions. I went to one called "The Genius of Thinking." It turns out that what makes someone a genius is not because they produce works of genius, like Mozart's sonatas, Beethoven's Symphony No. 9, or Picasso's *Girl Before a Mirror*. These masterpieces are a *consequence* of the genius of what these artists were thinking and feeling when they created their masterpieces.

The workshop exercise was to think about one of our greatest accomplishments and then unpack "What was I thinking?" that was the spark that produced the success. What was that voice in my head whispering and calling to me that inspired what became a work of my genius? What did that voice allow me to do differently that resulted in such a stupendous result? The theory is that if you can isolate that thought, then you can intentionally call it up again when you face your next opportunity to create magic and navigate through the imposter syndrome doubts of "Who do I think I am to…" You can move from magical thinking to thinking magically.

In the workshop, I thought about the nonprofit organi-zation that I co-founded with my dear friend Dr. Sylvia Ann Hewlett in 2005, The Center for Talent Innovation (now Coqual). Sylvia and I had the bold idea of bringing a second generation of policies and practices around gender equity, diversity, and inclusion into the corporate world. Our audacious goal was to heal the current talent management systems of their unconscious bias that influence the decisions of who gets hired, promoted, and listened to. By 2010, we had completed game-changing research, had three articles published in the *Harvard Business Review*, were supported by seventy-five of the leading companies in the world, and I was invited that year to be on the plenary stage at the MPW Summit to share some of our findings. What was the voice in my head, my genius of thinking?

As I thought about the creation of Coqual and some of my greatest breakthroughs over the decades, I was able to isolate my epic mantra: "What do you mean, No? Of course, I can!" "I can do this even though it hasn't been done before."

We women are biologically coded to be other-centric, drawn to the needs of others, willing to rise up and raise the level of our own play, our own genius of knowing, when the greater good is calling us. We stand on the shoulders of scores of women—Suffragettes, Abolitionists, Freedom Fighters— who defied the strictures of their station to fight in unseemly ways for a more peaceful, just, and fair existence for all.

The genius of our epic thinking and the willingness to play that out is the gift that keeps on giving. This insight was forever reinforced to me when my oldest son turned twenty-one. We went out drinking. Not his first time, but certainly mine with him. As we started on the second bottle of wine, I asked him what the impact had been on him that I had always worked outside the home.

I was particularly interested in his thoughts. Due to a benign but fast-growing tumor in his femur, he had not been weight bearing from the sixth to eighth grade, had five operations, and had been in a body cast three times. I continued working throughout this time, and he went to school, body cast and all. At night, as I washed his hair and rubbed his feet with peppermint oil, we would exchange stories about our day. After some eye-rolling, I assured him that I was asking him this question as a researcher, not his mom. This is what he told me. "Mom, I have a little voice in my ear that speaks to me when I am scared. It says, 'Go ahead. Take a risk. Good things happen when you do.' Mom, it's your voice." Like mother, like son.

EPIC! is just your genius of thinking. It is a choice you can make every day.

Final Tips

In previous chapters, I shared some of the components of my Decade Game 60–70. Here it is in its entirety. Although I start every decade with a new game board that I sketch out in an afternoon, it is my commitment to my mantra of "Of course I can do this!" that guides my choices of game moves.

Here are a few more tips that help you to stay on track as you play the game.

First, don't overthink it. Your game board should be like the main melody of a beautiful song, in five-part harmony. One that you can hum to yourself whenever you are stuck, scared, or confused. One that you can always remember the tune. To that end, like a great song, every word counts. Notice that my entire game board is only 101 words. Short and sweet. The words should fit together to tell an epic story, convey a longing, provide a clear direction, express a certain heart energy, illuminate a desired destiny. (Even as I write these words, I am struck by the irony that it takes me 46,000 words to write a book, the essence of which can be felt in 101 words!)

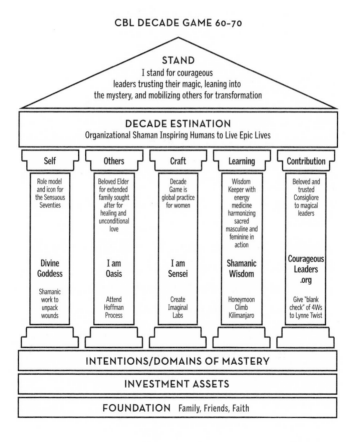

CBL DECADE GAME 60-70

STAND
I stand for courageous leaders trusting their magic, leaning into the mystery, and mobilizing others for transformation

DECADE ESTINATION
Organizational Shaman Inspiring Humans to Live Epic Lives

Self	Others	Craft	Learning	Contribution
Role model and icon for the Sensuous Seventies	Beloved Elder for extended family sought after for healing and unconditional love	Decade Game is global practice for women	Wisdom Keeper with energy medicine harmonizing sacred masculine and feminine in action	Beloved and trusted Consigliore to magical leaders
Divine Goddess	**I am Oasis**	**I am Sensei**	**Shamanic Wisdom**	**Courageous Leaders .org**
Shamanic work to unpack wounds	Attend Hoffman Process	Create Imaginal Labs	Honeymoon Climb Kilimanjaro	Give "blank check" of 4Ws to Lynne Twist

INTENTIONS/DOMAINS OF MASTERY

INVESTMENT ASSETS

FOUNDATION Family, Friends, Faith

Second, develop mantras or axioms that remind you to center yourself back into playing your game over the years. I have created axioms that remind me of how to keep my mindset and game face operating, particularly in the face of the constant cultural pushback against ambitious women. Axiom is another word for norms that define "the way things are" today. Today's accepted axioms best reflect what has worked for the majority who are privileged in our culture and society—white, straight, adult men. The Decade Game turns many of these traditional axioms upside down to unleash women and other historically underrepresented groups to play a game of their own design, with their rules, that work in both the good and difficult times.

These axioms serve as favorite tunes that I can sing to myself when I'm stuck, triggered, or at a decision crossroads. My experience is that "Good Girls" suffer when they are not sure of what the right move is in a situation and are afraid of not being seen as highly competent in their job. When I am agonizing over what a good mother or trusted colleague would do in a particular situation, my Decade Game board might not be sufficient in that moment. This is when I rely on my songbook of axioms.

Here are some of the axioms that whisper in my ear and guide my play. They are the new rules of the game.

Create your life by design, not default. You have all the assets you need—tangible and intangible—to have a life of meaning and purpose. And you are in control of the design parameters, no one else. You are the master

designer able to create your own personal design based on your unique circumstances. You can iterate toward the best fit of both today's realities and tomorrow's dreams. Don't give up your power and authority to old stories.

 **Practice thoughtful wishing instead of wishful thinking:** Many people live in the past "I shoulda, woulda, coulda" or in the future "I really wish…" but aren't willing to take committed action for that desire. That is wishful thinking. On the other hand, if you practice "Want what you have, do what you can, and be who you are," you have all that you need to have a life filled with meaning, purpose, and gratitude. That is thoughtful wishing. And unlike wishful thinking, thoughtful wishes always come true.

You can't get there from here, but you can get here from there: The most effective way to manifest a transformation is by fully imagining and prototyping what *might be*—the *"there"*—and transporting as much of the star stuff of that future state as possible back into today's reality. The magic of our brain/ heart partnership is that all you need to do is to fully claim and commit to that future vision of yourself, and the work of transformation has already begun. And remember, "If you know where you are going, any road will get you there."

 There is no such thing as bad weather, only the wrong clothes: We can imagine a decade destination and build a blueprint to guide our choices. However, we have no idea what the real itinerary will be. Often the breakthrough happens after an unplanned break-down. We can blame it on mother nature, force majeure, bad luck, inclement circumstances beyond our control. Or we can change our clothes, attitudes, and understanding of the underlying problem and repack appropriately to take advantage of where we find ourselves with our destination firmly in our hearts.

If you aren't part of the problem, you can't be part of the solution: The Decade Game has less to do with knowing the right answer and fixing stuff than it does empa- thetically leaning into what is longing to become right. There is also a gentle, nonjudgmental, forgiving quality to the jour-ney. A rear-view decade-long mirror honors all that has happened that has gotten you to this point. Both the traumas and the triumphs of the past become the treasures to equip you for the best decade of your life so far.

 If you can't have fun with a problem, you can never solve it: The secret sauce of the Decade Game is that it is a game of "broccoli-covered chocolate" instead of "chocolate-covered broccoli." The work of designing a transformational life is hard work—and you need to eat all your broccoli. Putting challenging ideas into play and laughing and dancing with the ideas in a brave space of your own choosing allows you to show up with all your God-given gifts. You discover that it's the sweet choc-olate that has always been inside you that is the secret ingredient.

If you are not having fun, you are playing someone else's game: Play brings out people's greatest creativity and imagination. It reduces their fear of losing. The "move is not the game." And there is no such thing as a wrong move in the Decade Game. It is a continual learning experience of how to play your game better. The more challenging a game—the more fun it is to play, even when it is hard, sweaty, tearful work. If your life is not fun and feeling full of meaning, then you are most likely playing by someone else's rules.

 **When in Rome, do as the Romanians do:** This axiom needs a little more explanation! I was once on a business trip about to take off from Newark airport to Rome. Two women leisure travelers sitting behind me were so excited. About to toast each other with champagne, one said to the other, "When in Rome, do as the Romanians do." In the Decade Game, you are creating a new identity that expresses your greatest dreams and aspirations, which are unique to you. There has NEVER in history been anyone that has had the same fingerprint, eye pigmentation, and vocal tone that you do. Therefore no one will do, see, or voice your truth, other than you. Create your own identity that unleashes your full imagination. Be a unique traveler.

It is not who you know—it is how you are known for the way you love.  Many women have an ambivalent relationship to ambition. Instead of the often seen "hero archetype" of "Speak Loudly and Carry a Big Stick," women dream big yet play small. Your epic Decade Game destination asks players to imagine how they will be known in the world. This requires you to build a strong brand. Your brand is based on how other people feel when they engage with you. At its essence, it is about how you love. Make sure you are not your best-kept secret.

 The power of a positive "no." Women in their "Good Girl" mindset have a hard time creating the boundaries of what they want and desire. They say "yes" in order not to displease. There is a way to say "no" that is affirming to both the woman and the person they are saying "no" to. Knowing who you are becoming, what it means to really be in right relationship with Others, and to be clear about your overall desired decade identity helps you with the power of a positive "no."

Honor the Resistance—Resistance is Futile. Resistance builds muscle. We welcome it, however painful. Resistance to an epic life is an alert for what is longing to happen—whether it's mending a rift with a colleague or loved one, deciding to "go for it," asking for help, or saying "yes" to you. Resistance is a sign of energy, longing to be released. Honor and then fight the antibodies in our culture against "epic-ness." We were raised to be "Good Girls" navigating the tightrope of "too this/ too that." Resistance signals fear of failure and judgment, not fear of transformation. And what you resist, persists. As the chief designer of the new rules, you are in control. Resistance is futile.

Be totally present and totally ready—Level 10 thinking and Level 1 doing. Often, we don't show up fully present because we are worried about the "next steps," "the next promotion," or "What if they think I am…" You will do your best work and have your greatest impact if you bring the awareness of your Level 10 intentions into the task and relationships in front of you. Yet, when the next best step emerges out of the universe, you KNOW it is right and won't let the doubts of the past influence your decision to act.

Invest wisely in the rule of three. Any initiative, project, or action you take on—organize it in a way that allows you to make progress and deepen your learning on three of five pillars of your Decade Game at the same time. This creates an integrated exponential energy toward your commitment to mastery and your decade destination. Your pillars become a force multiplier. Remember, your job is not what you are being paid to do. It is to become a savvy investor in the experiences, knowledge, and relationships that fuel your overarching purpose.

The trials and tribulations of the past are the treasures that fund the future. No one can predict the future—either next week or next year. Knowing the future is not necessary. The real game is to be equipped—emotionally, spiritually, and physically—to embrace an uncertain future, knowing that we all have everything we need at this moment to discover what is the next best move. We have the gifts of hindsight, forgiveness, resilience, and gratitude that come from all the highs and lows, the trials and triumphs as individuals and society—and they are the treasures that fund our future.

An epic life worth living is an off-road journey. We have not been trained to live off-road. We have been taught to be linear thinkers, with the future being an extrapolation of the past. We have been trained to believe and trust in "cause and effect"—that we can trace outcomes back to what caused them. In our family budgets and organizational plans, we build projections and predictions for what we estimate the future will hold based on a study of past and present trends. It's not our fault. Our brains think this way as well. Living an epic life is venturing into the unknown, trusting in what is longing to happen and our authentic gifts that are always with us on the journey.

The choice to be epic is always within reach. It is inside you, lying in wait for you to call it forth and give it voice. You have the power of the universe inside you, listening for what is longing to happen. Reach for your purpose, on purpose.

Are you ready to play?

Game On.

Epilogue

1,000 Sundays

I t was a beautiful late winter day in late February 2013 in San Rafael, CA—fifty-five degrees, not a cloud in the sky, brisk with hints of summer warmth. My husband and I had just parked in the lot by the magnificent Marin County Civic Center built by Frank Lloyd Wright. We walked down the hill into what looked like an eighteenth-century village fair—The Sunday Farmer's market of Marin. It was a sea of covered stalls, waves of wonderful smells, children playing, families milling, neighbors catching up on the news. As I surveyed the scene below me and the beautiful Lucas Valley Hills beyond, I thought about how blessed I was to be able to make market Sunday into a new tradition.

It was my first Sunday at the market. We were back from our honeymoon climbing Mt. Kilimanjaro and had just moved into our new home in Upper Lucas Valley, a mid-century marvel built by Joseph Eichler, a student of Frank Lloyd Wright. It was a big change for me being that I was a NYC girl, having lived there for thirty-eight years and having spent my entire sixty years on the East Coast. However, the advent of my sixtieth birthday in 2012 had brought on major life changes—not as a late-life crisis—but as the ending of a great chapter and the beginning of the last quartile of my life. In December 2012, I had gotten married, retired after two decades from the partnership of Ernst & Young, bought the San Rafael house, and was starting my next Decade Game from sixty to seventy.

Looking down on the market, I was transported to that long-past time, when local farmers, artisans, craftsmen, journeymen, and families would come together to exchange goods and gossip. It felt timeless. Time is a funny thing. While you are in it, time can seem endless. And then it can seem over in the blink of an eye. While climbing Mt. Kilimanjaro, I had a lot of time to think about time. When you are struggling to climb twelve hours a day in high altitudes at forty-five-degree angles, the hours stretch forever as you can only focus on each step. In fact, my husband, ever the wise teacher, gave us a mantra that was essential to our ascent—"Every step our hearts get stronger, every step our lungs get stronger, every step our legs get stronger, every step our love gets stronger."

This experience gave me the opportunity to live the time continuum, simultaneously thinking about the next Decade Game as well as the interminable length of each sixty seconds, step by step. And it gave me time to do math in my head. Instead of counting sheep, I counted time.

I was obviously very conversant with how many hours are in ten years—87,600 hours, to be exact. Part of my decade "theory of change" is that you have the golden opportunity to be very intentional in how you choose to invest the 50,000 hours that you are awake in building the experiences, knowledge, and relationships that allow you to live your life in a manner worth dying for.

I had a surprising and sobering realization during the 300,000 seconds of climbing twelve hours a day for a week. At sixty and reasonably healthy, barring any unseen circumstances over which I have no control, my life expectancy should take me to at least the age of eighty with a decent quality of life. With my focus on my next Decade Game for my sixties, I hadn't really done the math about the rest of my life. The temporal depth and breadth of the math I did on the mountain gave me another very important perspective on time. I might have only 1,000 Sundays left. Time to make every second count.

> If you can fill the unforgiving minute
> With sixty seconds' worth of distance run,
> Yours is the Earth and everything that's in it.
> And—which is more—you'll be a [Hu]man, my son!
> —RUDYARD KIPLING FROM THE POEM *IF*

At the time I write this, I am sixty-nine, and my mother is ninety-three. So maybe I have 1,500 Sundays left. I have only one year left in my Decade Game 60–70 as an Organizational Shaman and am already thinking about formulating my next Decade Game. How will I know myself and be known by the people I love and who count on me when I am eighty? What will the next imaginal stage of my metamorphosis look and feel like? How does a mature Elder show up in the world?

On the other hand, maybe I have only one hundred

Sundays left. Life is filled with trap doors. We will never be able to predict the end of the story—for our loved ones or us. However, we are living now in the middle of our stories, and we will leave this life in the middle of the stories of the people we love. No matter when the curtain comes down, if we have lived life as fully as we can, if we have been able to throw our hearts into the service of others, we will have forever shaped the plot as well as the character of our beloved characters.

Now that is EPIC!

Acknowledgments

Over the last fifty of my seventy years, many people, upon hearing my stories, have said, "Oh! You HAVE to write a book." This book, however, is not about me. It is about what is longing to happen in the hearts and lives of women who I have walked with in all my different roles at home, at work, and in the world. I have them and their encouragement to thank for EPIC!.

One of the blessings of being seventy is that there are legions of people, too many to enumerate, that have indelibly imprinted my character and plotlines. There are a few of these angels that I would like to specifically acknowledge here.

To my great teacher and friend, Lynne Twist, whose own life helped me reimagine mine.

To Sara Vetter and Tracy Maes, who welcomed me into the leadership team of the Remarkable Women's Journey.

To Lisa DeCarlo and Tina Staley, who believed enough in the power of the Decade Game to devote their precious time and wisdom to bring it to the world.

To the REMARKABLES and Decade Gamers—you know who you are—who trusted me to help them trust their EPIC!.

To my EPIC! Women's Launch Council, who dedicated their time and wisdom to make sure this book would get into the right hands and hearts.

To my team at Scribe Media, who guided and supported me through all the twists and turns of the changing publishing world.

And last but not least, to my family.

My mother, Minna Buck, who has inspired me all my life with her selfless service to others.

My siblings, Beverly and Michael Buck, who have been with me since the beginning.

My beloved sons, Jacob and Nathan, who have loved me "no matter what" since their beginning.

My cherished children by marriage—Frank, Nina, Jonah, and Abby—who have made a place for me at their tables.

My treasured grandchildren—Jamie, Emily, Lincoln, Helen, Beatrix, Maxine, and Arthur—to whom I pour all my hopes and dreams.

And to my darling, Rob, who will see me through to the end of my story.